On Fly-Fishing the
NORTHERN
ROCKIES

On Fly-Fishing the
NORTHERN ROCKIES

Essays and Dubious Advice

CHADD VANZANTEN & RUSS BECK

THE
History
PRESS

Published by The History Press
Charleston, SC 29403
www.historypress.net

Front cover: Wind Rivers Range. *Courtesy of Chadd VanZanten.*
Back cover, bottom: The Blonde Torpedo of Destiny stalks brookies.
Courtesy of Chadd VanZanten.

All images provided by the authors unless otherwise noted.

First published 2015

Manufactured in the United States

ISBN 978.1.46711.801.9

Library of Congress Control Number: 2015937272

Notice: The information in this book is true and complete to the best of our knowledge. It is offered without guarantee on the part of the authors or The History Press. The authors and The History Press disclaim all liability in connection with the use of this book.

Russ would like to dedicate this book to Rocket and Rocket Jr. You're both my very favorite.

Chadd dedicates this book to Amanda.

CONTENTS

Acknowledgements   9

RULE 1: IF YOU'RE NOT GOING TO FISH ALONE, YOU SHOULD
   PROBABLY BRING SOMEONE WITH YOU
   An Act of Mercy: Russ Beck   13
   Almost Always Enough: Chadd VanZanten   17
   The Mighty Mo Don't Care: Russ Beck   22
   Then Came November: Chadd VanZanten   26

RULE 2: FISH WHERE YOU'RE AT
   A Good Place to Make Saints: Russ Beck   31
   In the Fortress of the Sandhill Crane: Chadd VanZanten   35
   America's Caveat River: Russ Beck   39

RULE 3: FISH WHERE YOU END UP
   The Places We End Up At: Chadd VanZanten   43
   American and Canadian Football: Russ Beck   47
   Terrestrials Adrift: Chadd VanZanten   51

RULE 4: ALL THE FISH ARE UNDER WATER
   All the Fish Are Under Water: Chadd VanZanten   57
   Where They Aren't: Chadd VanZanten   61

CONTENTS

RULE 5: AND HE SAITH UNTO THEM, FOLLOW ME, AND I WILL MAKE YOU FISHERS OF MEN (MATTHEW 4:19)
Belief, Luck and Lies: Russ Beck 65

RULE 6: SIMON PETER SAITH UNTO THEM, I GO A FISHING, THEY SAY UNTO HIM, WE ALSO GO WITH THEE, THEY WENT FORTH AND ENTERED INTO A SHIP IMMEDIATELY AND THAT NIGHT THEY CAUGHT NOTHING (JOHN 21:3)
The Iron Rod: Russ Beck 71

RULE 7: YOUR PLAN? IT SUCKS
Final Plan F: Chadd VanZanten 79
They're Always for Me: Russ Beck 87

RULE 8: MAYBE YOUR STATURE AS A FLY FISHERMAN ISN'T DETERMINED BY HOW BIG A TROUT YOU CAN CATCH BUT BY HOW SMALL A TROUT YOU CAN CATCH WITHOUT BEING DISAPPOINTED (JOHN GIERACH)
How Small a Trout: Russ Beck 91
A Very Small Stream: Chadd VanZanten 95

RULE 9: ALWAYS TELL THE TRUTH SOMETIMES
Always Tell the Truth Sometimes: Russ Beck 99
Toward the Wilder Places: Chadd VanZanten 104

Appendix A: On Various Catch Totals and Their Significance, by Chadd VanZanten 109
Appendix B: The Essay in Which the Author Compares People to Trout, by Russ Beck 115
Appendix C: A Partial Checklist for Fishing Alone, by Chadd VanZanten and Russ Beck 121
About the Authors 125

ACKNOWLEDGEMENTS

We give deepest thanks to Artie Crisp of The History Press for his patience and invaluable support in the risky proposition of giving birth to this book. Thanks also go to Bradley Hansen, who not only confidently predicted the existence of this book years before the idea occurred to either of us, but who also showed the way to many of the places mentioned herein, and to everyone who has ever been associated with Roundrocks Fly Fishing—owners, guides, part-time shop guys, full-time scoundrels, mentors, fibbers and heroes. We learned a little from each of you.

We take our place among the scores of writers who bear a debt of gratitude to Star Coulbrooke.

RUSS

I would like to thank Kacy Lundstrom and Henrietta Beck, who spent many weekends quietly waiting for me to come home, first because I was fishing and living these stories (blame Brad or Chadd or Jason for my getting home late) and then because I was writing these essays. I'm one lucky jerk. Boyd and Sandra Beck not only curated some of the photographs within but also, well, raised me. They've always supported me, even when they didn't fully understand my interests (be they music, fishing, board games or this whole writing thing). I thank all my fishing and writing buddies: Kevin Larsen, Andrew Davidson, Dr. Lynne S. McNeil, Dr. Stephen VanGeem, Russ Winn, Pamela Martin Stohosky, Nathan Stohosky, Maure Smith-Benanti, Dustin Crawford, Jason Reed, Kirk Benge, Kirk Watson, Clinto Watson, Dylan Klempner (who believed in this book long before I ever did), Elizabeth Andrews, Meredith May, Mora Finnerty, Nancy Sharp, Jacoba Poppleton, E-beth Benson, Jackie Harris, Emily Grover, Darren Edwards, Matt Lavin, Ben Quick, Liz Stephens, Kelsey Osgood, Brian Mockenhaupt, Patrick Walters, Ly Nguyen, Sarah Wolfgang, Brian Spadora, Tracey Emslie, Eleanor Hogan, Jennifer Lapidus, Melinda Copp, Daniel Higgins, Amri Brown and Joel Karpowitz. I'm also grateful for all the writing mentors I've had over the years, starting at Snow College with Jeff Carney, Ron Lamb, Melanie Jenkins, David Rosier and Steve Peterson; then at BYU with John Bennion; next at USU with Chris Cokinos, Jennifer Sinor and Charles Waugh; and finally at Goucher College with Patsy Sims, Kevin Kerrane, Leslie Rubinkowski, Dick Todd and Diana Hume George, who taught me the valuable lesson that there should be no bullshit between English teachers.

CHADD

I would like to thank and acknowledge my ever-astonishing offspring—Shreve, Ingrid, Gretchen and Klaus—whom Russ Beck once observed are "all real people." He was more correct than he knew—you guys are the realest thing that has ever happened in the history of things happening. Thanks go to Jason Reed and the Blonde Torpedo of Destiny for tireless fishing companionship and friendly groin nuzzling, respectively (usually). To Pete Tyjas of Eat Sleep Fish, thank you for giving my writing a place to hang out for a while. Sincere thanks go to Tim Keller and my writing group: Amber, Aaron, Ben, Britney, Danette, Dianne, Dustin, Emily, Felicia, Isaac, the Other Jeff, the Original Jeff, Jeremy, Lynne, Neil, Robyn, Turbo and Sherrie Lynn. No less sincere thanks go to my first writing group: Carrie Anne, Daniel, Darren, E-beth, Emily, Jackie, Kacy and Sarah. And stretching even further into the past, thank you Jay Wamsley and Sandra Turner for teaching me about English. To Tim King, thank you for teaching me to fish, tie and tell stories. Special thanks go to Amanda Luzzader, editor, colleague, source of unflagging encouragement and best friend.

ACKNOWLEDGEMENTS

Henrietta Jane, Kacy and Russ.

RUSS WOULD LIKE TO THANK Chadd for his fishing advice and friendship. Chadd would like to say, "You are very welcome, sir. And thanks to you also for your advice on writing," to which Russ would like to reply, "It's no problem, man, but I've been meaning to ask you—did you ever return my tenkara rod? That Iwana?" In response Chadd answers, "Yes, for the last time, we switched rods. Remember? You have mine. I have yours. You want yours back? Do you really think it's worth it to switch back now, you petty son of a bitch? It's been two years already."

ACKNOWLEDGEMENTS

"Well, it has sentimental value."

"Sentimental value? It's a piece of carbon."

"Never mind. I've replaced four sections in the one I have. I'll just keep it."

"Four sections? Well, maybe we should switch back. You know. Sentimental value and all that."

Russ Beck would like to recommend that Chadd go to hell.

Rule 1

IF YOU'RE NOT GOING TO FISH ALONE, YOU SHOULD PROBABLY BRING SOMEONE WITH YOU

AN ACT OF MERCY

Russ Beck

I nearly bailed the first time Chadd invited me to fly-fish with him. I told him I had a cold, but he guilted me into it anyway.

"You know I don't mind going on my own. If you've got a cold, that's cool, but I was looking forward to going with someone."

I did have an inkling of a cold: a tickle in the back of the back of my throat. But the real reason I didn't want to go fly-fishing was because I had never been before. Sure, I had spin-fished for a large chunk of my life, but my fly-fishing skills were nonexistent. I practiced casting on my back lawn for hours, but I figured making the fly line snap was a good thing. I thought making the leader fray only happened when you used a lot of power. I knew enough to know that I didn't know anything.

But I went. I met him at Second Dam on Logan River on an early November afternoon. Fall couldn't decide if it was staying or leaving. The leaves, dark brown or gone, hung above the clear and low water. We started at the reservoir, casting to fish that rose to midges. I decided my best bet was to pretend that I knew what I was doing.

After my second attempt at casting, Chadd said, "Maybe you should just watch for a while."

I did. I noticed that although his fly line looked graceful and never stopped moving, his rod jerked with starts and stops. I watched Chadd's line open up at the end and place the fly on the water gently. It didn't make sense. So I watched some more. Then I tried again—but I shouldn't have.

We moved from the still water to some riffles upstream and tried nymphing. I realize now this was an act of mercy. He probably thought that I'd be able to better handle the short casts. He was wrong. We cast to a hole next to the bank where we could see fish actively feeding.

He said, "Cast as close to the bank as you can without hitting it."

I tried and hit the bank. My line tangled in the root system of a tree leaning over the hole. I had to walk right through the fish to retrieve my fly and line.

"I don't know how to say this," Chadd said, "so I'm just going to come out with it: have you ever caught a fish on a fly rod?"

I'm not sure why now, but I was embarrassed. With my facial hair, large stature and closet filled with flannel and wool, I felt like I needed a reason for not catching a fish on a fly rod this late in my life, but I had none. I hemmed and hawed for a bit and eventually said no. He nodded. I think he knew the answer to his question before he asked it.

"How did you do it? How did you get so good?" I asked.

"I'm not good." He was tying a Glo-Bug on the end of my line and paused to put the tippet in his mouth to lubricate the knot. "You'll see people who can throw all their line without thinking about it. I learned by coming up here and messing up, by getting caught up in that root system." He pointed to the spot where I had just got snagged. "And that tree, and that one." He pointed up the river.

"But you catch fish."

"Yeah. I catch fish."

I shrugged and waited for him to talk again.

"You'll catch fish, too. You've got to catch your first. You've got to get the proof-of-concept fish. Then it will all make sense."

As a response, I threw a cast that tangled onto the bank. My Glo-Bug wrapped around my indicator. When I retrieved the mess, the split shot dangled down like a broken clock's pendulum.

He watched as I tried to untangle the jumble.

"You know what you need to do? Find an angler. Like one of those friends you mentioned earlier. Someone who knows what they're doing, someone who doesn't throw a tailing loop, and you need to stitch yourself to his back pocket. Ask him questions and buy him breakfast and find out when he's going fishing and just show up."

My guides clogged with ice, and my net froze and stuck to my back.

He emphasized the words that distanced him from me. The ones that made me know that he wasn't offering to be my fishing mentor.

"What's a 'tailing loop'?" I asked.

"Exactly. Ask things like that."

A week later, winter came, and I met Chadd on the same river at the same time. My guides clogged with ice, and my net froze and stuck to my back. Without warning or ceremony, eventually I caught a fish. A brown much bigger than he should have been for my first fish on a fly. It was a short cast, maybe six feet under a footbridge. The split shot hit the water first and in front of my egg pattern. Chadd worked a side channel about twenty yards away from me. I thought about keeping him in the net and taking him to Chadd—somehow offering the fish as proof or a sacrifice or a tax or something else that I didn't understand because I was new to this. It felt like there needed to be some sort of ceremony with fanfare and pomp.

But of course, there wasn't any of that, and I didn't do any of that. Instead, I pulled the fish in and admired his exaggerated spots and golden belly. His gill plates moved up and down slowly, matching my own breathing. I cupped the fish in my bare hands and slid him back into the cold water.

Chadd was right. After I got my proof-of-concept fish, everything started to change and make sense. I spent every hour I could on a stream. My casts became sharp, accurate and tight. I learned to roll cast, and watching that line open up like a time-lapse recording of a flower blossoming was one of the most satisfying images of my adult life. I began to mend the line before

I thought about keeping him in the net and taking him to Chadd—somehow offering the fish as proof or a sacrifice or a tax or something else that I didn't understand because I was new to this. It felt like there needed to be some sort of ceremony with fanfare and pomp.

I knew what "mend the line" meant. And most importantly, I caught more fish. I'm still not good, but I'm competent.

Back to that wintry November day. After a couple of hours on the water, we called it quits. I ended the day with that single brown—Chadd had around twenty, but that's a guess. As an act of kindness, he didn't give me an actual number. As we walked back to our cars, I remember hitting my hands on my thighs to get feeling back in my fingers. We talked and laughed. Mostly about how horrible I was at fishing. We went to breakfast at a local diner to warm up. When the check came, I picked up the tab.

ALMOST ALWAYS ENOUGH

Chadd VanZanten

Mild desperation drove me to winter fishing. I used to quit in the fall. Then one year, November lumbered up, and I wasn't ready to put my gear away. So I didn't. I kept going out, almost every week.

That first winter I fished alone, and I didn't have a lot of experience. I might have caught two fish and at least that many colds. But I found something else out there that kept me going back—the twisted sense of accomplishment of doing something other people consider crazy. It's what made Evel Knieval jump the Snake River. It's why Bear Grylls drinks his own pee on TV from time to time.

Fishing through western winters sharpens the angler, too. It advances his rank. I'm not talking about fishing an Indian summer or a bright afternoon in late February. I mean fishing in hard mountain cold, grinding through icy weeks of January in search of one decent snowfly hatch. It's a way to earn stripes.

That's why I invited Russ along for the first time, not for the companionship but so that he could come and see how much of a badass I was and then spread my legend among the townsfolk. What good are stripes when there's no one around to salute you?

I knew he wouldn't show because I set an irrationally early start time. The conventional wisdom of winter fishing says hold off until the sun comes out. Something about letting the fish warm up. Like they're senior citizens in a water aerobics class. I knew better. Waiting around for the sun to shine on the Logan River is a good way to get yourself skunked, so I typically start around 9:30 a.m. I told Russ we'd meet at 8:30 to see if he'd show at all. I guess that's what happens when you start acting tough—you give your friends these silly tests.

In my defense, I never had many fishing buddies before that. I had been fly-fishing for less than ten years and almost always fished alone. I'd asked a few guys to come winter fishing with me, but most of them did the right thing—laughed nervously and held out their hands.

Until Russ came along, only two other guys had ever said yes to my winter fishing overtures—Tom and Robert, a couple guys from the office where I work. Robert's from South Carolina; Tom's from Florida. I don't know what they were thinking. I really do not. Maybe they thought they harbored some special inner heat sources from their native climes. Maybe they were just calling my bluff. We fished in the afternoon, against my better judgment, but the day was cold anyway, with harsh winds, much ice and no fish. In other words, just a typical page from my badass winter fishing journal. I still see Tom and Robert around the office, but they don't talk to me much anymore.

Russ and I had gotten to be friends, so I felt it a shame that the matter of winter fishing would soon come between us, too. But the invitation was out there, and Russ had already accepted.

Even though it was supposed to snow that day, Russ said, "OK. I'll go. Unless I look out the window in the morning and it's like, oh hell no."

When I pulled up to the riverside turnout and saw Russ's car already there, I justifiably assumed someone who looked just like Russ had stolen the car and was on the lam in the canyon. I didn't want to blow his cover, so I parked and unpacked my waders without saying anything.

Russ strolled over, ready to go, as I suited up.

"Cold?" I asked.

He looked around as if the temperature had just occurred to him. Then he shrugged. "I'm OK."

"Well, wait till we get out there," I said, jerking my chin at the water. I may have made my voice extra gravelly, like Quint from *Jaws* or George C. Scott in *Patton*. I'm not sure what kept me from saying, "Y'ever hook a big German brown with ice in all yer guides, son?"

We fished. Russ didn't catch much, which is to say he didn't catch anything. Then it sleeted on us a little.

After an hour, I asked, "How you doing now?"

"I should probably get some good gloves," said Russ, flexing his stiff, bare fingers. "Like yours."

I still have the gloves he was referring to—fingerless fleece with neoprene palms and mitten tops that fold back. They're fuzzy and bulky and make me look like I've got Mickey Mouse hands. They weren't very warm when they were new, and they were starting to come apart. Some really nice ones had been showing up at the shops. But they were kind of expensive, and I thought buying a pair might be construed as an admission that the cold bothered me. After Russ pointed out that I had gloves and he didn't, I considered tossing mine into the river to eliminate his handicap but thought better of it.

After a while, I couldn't go winter fishing without Russ. The colder it got, the harder that guy fished. Watching him brave the conditions became a sort of heat source for me. He fished without gloves for at least the first month. He'd just sniff and shake his hands every so often. I didn't tell him that I normally fished for only an hour or two when it was really cold like it was that year. That was my secret—I'm no badass. Any fool can dress up warm

We had some good days, and some really good days, but then the browns quit spawning and February arrived and we couldn't find a trout in the whole river.

and stand in the water for an hour, especially if his hands aren't wet from catching lots of fish.

Maybe that was Russ's secret—his casting ensured that his hands were dry a lot of the time. This made it tricky to decide if he was having any fun, and I strongly suspected he wasn't. I got the feeling he kept showing up to call the bluff over and over, to prove he wasn't a wimp. We had some good days and some really good days, but then the browns quit spawning and February arrived and we couldn't find a trout in the whole river.

I thought finally Russ would start staying home, so I told him this: "Sometimes it's just good enough to get out."

Yeah, that old chestnut. We all say it, especially after getting skunked. I've always had a hard time believing it. The Logan River is home to one of the largest populations of wild, native cutthroat trout in the world. Anyone who has held a fine, heavy fish from that population knows it's slightly blasphemous to say, "It's not about the fish," but at that moment, it was the only thing I could think of.

Crazy thing is, Russ bought it. Or he already knew it. He was never all that broken up when he caught no fish. He'd just shrug and flex his hands. Sometimes, when he should have been casting, I'd catch him standing still, just scanning the river and the willow brake with its naked, waxy branches crowding along the cold water. He'd stand there watching, as though the trout (caught or otherwise) were just one part of some greater observance.

He could have just as well have been exhibiting the early symptoms of hypothermia, I suppose.

Either way, Russ got me thinking that as improbable as it seemed, maybe I was actually right. Maybe there is enough out there to take in apart from fish. Mule deer barely glimpsed before blending against a field of last summer's cattails. Big glassy bells of ice dangling from branches that droop into the current. I'll admit there are days when such sights are as pleasing as the fish I catch.

Always impressive to me is the lone ouzel hunting in thirty-eight-degree water. He titters up alongside me, does a few quick knee-bends and regards me with one eye. Then he moves on. If I am an odd or unwelcome sight in the winter landscape, the ouzel does not make it known, yet I feel I am there because he has decided to allow it.

In spring, summer and fall, it's difficult to have any western waterway to yourself, even for an hour. Rivers exert an irresistible gravitational force on those who live nearby. All through the sensible seasons, everyone's got an excuse to visit a river—got a new dog, holiday weekend, friends in town. The mere appearance of the sun after a day of rain in May can be ruinous to an angler's chance for solitude. In spring and fall, there are places along the Logan River where you are more likely to see a young lady in a bridal gown and her photographer than a moose or beaver.

In January, that all changes. The river in winter is viewed as desolate, hazardous even, and for nine weeks or ten, it becomes possible to own vast stretches of water as if you hold an actual deed.

A solitary angler on the river in February is an odd and unwelcome sight to me. But I pretend to allow it. His wife and friends think he's a fool, and maybe he is. But I know he just wants the water to himself. So, I wave to him but keep my distance. He waves back—probably thinking all the same things about me. I wonder if he had to fish alone in the freezing river for a couple winters to earn his first fishing buddy and if that buddy helped him understand that getting out there is almost always enough.

This winter Russ got some new gloves—really nice ones. Windproof but light and not nearly so bulky as mine. He says they're warm. They look expensive.

After a while, I couldn't go winter fishing without Russ. The colder it got, the harder that guy fished.

THE MIGHTY MO DON'T CARE

Russ Beck

Brad's wife, Janelle, worked with Chadd and told him that Brad needed some new fishing buddies. She said she didn't trust the ones he had—they stayed out too late, they never checked in or something like that. So we all first met in a Walmart parking lot to carpool up to southern Idaho to fish the Oneida Narrows section of the Bear River.

Brad wore a camo ball cap and sunglasses. He looked like he was trying not to be recognized, like he was stepping out. His wiry frame jerked his gear out of his Jeep and tossed it in the back of my car with a certain disregard that seemed off for a fly angler.

We exchanged awkward salutations and moved to our conversational common ground: fly-fishing. We talked about fly patterns, hatches and risers. He said he had really been fly-fishing for only a few months. Despite his inexperience, I decided to try to treat him like an equal, but I pictured laughing gently as I untangled his line or chiding him with a finger wag and an admonition to do better next time.

When we got out of the car, Brad yanked on his neoprene-duck waders and put together his department store rod. He pulled a tattered vest down over his head.

Chadd laughed, "You know they come with zippers, Bradley."

"My zipper got stuck last time. So, I have to do it like this." He looked like a toddler trying on clothes that no longer fit.

Once he got the vest situated, he tossed his net over his shoulder (he didn't have a magnetic net stay; instead, he wrapped the spent elastic line around his body). He dispensed with the courtesy of fussing with his gear while the rest of us threaded our guides and pulled on boots. Instead, he jogged to the river and caught three fish before I even tied a fly on.

"What you using there?" I asked as I watched him net his fourth fish.

"Something. Not sure. It's shiny and heavy."

He pulled out his line and showed me a bead-head nymph. It looked like a variation on a Prince Nymph. I wasn't sure if he was playing dumb or if he really couldn't recognize a Prince Nymph.

There was something vulgar about the way Brad nymphed. His casts were ugly, short and purposeful. Instead of the even ebb and flow that I tried to mimic in my own fishing, Brad was all about quick starts and stops. Weeks later, I would find out (not from him) that his style was a bastardized version of Euro-nymphing. He cast with two hands; his line didn't even make it out of the top guide, and the leader was so stiff it swung rather than looped. It was fly-fishing in name only.

If they made a movie about Brad, Brad Pitt would not play him—not because they don't look anything alike but because Pitt couldn't make what Brad did look good, and Pitt won't be in any movie where he doesn't look good.

"Are you using an indicator?"

"This?" he yanked on his line and showed me a small red-and-white sleeve pulled over his leader. "I stripped the housing off some electrical wires. It works OK."

Brad outfished me that day and nearly every other time I fished with him—which ended up being at least once, usually twice, sometimes three times a week for about two years. I'm not sure what Janelle was looking for in buddies for Brad, but I'm pretty sure it wasn't us.

Before he moved, Brad and I met up a few times to tie flies or to go to Trout Unlimited meetings, but that's as far away as we got from the river. I'd fished with him four or five times before I even realized he worked on the same college campus as me and in the same building as my wife. It was months before I saw him without polarized sunglasses. He was carrying a stack of papers and rushing between buildings on campus. His eye color surprised me.

It was after a year of fishing together that I learned he was a musician. Later, I learned he was struggling with his faith. We skipped the small things like God and politics and talked only about the important things like the ideal length of tippet between a fly and an indicator.

It was embarrassing to fish with Brad because he was so damn good with so little. I spent thousands where he spent hundreds. I would have avoided fishing with him if he hadn't been so humble. And he was excited about every fish caught, especially the fish I caught. Plus, he made me a better, more hungry angler.

Once, on the Blacksmith Fork River, he walked up behind me and said, "You want to know how to get at that guy?"

"Which guy?"

"That fish you keep just missing. You need to—well, do you want me to show you?"

He slung his line into a hole I didn't see, and he mended his line back so there was no drag—and connected with a decent brown.

He didn't get this good on accident. His fishing schedule was exhausting. He found ways to fish before and after work, sometimes even on his lunch break. His haggard dedication to the sport was admirable, but it eroded other parts of his life. The holes he created by angling were filled with fish. Janelle mentioned to Chadd that it was beyond an obsession—she thought that he spent entirely too much time on the river. I didn't want to, but I agreed with Janelle. Brad mentioned to me in passing that they were visiting a marriage counselor.

I knew Cache Valley couldn't keep Brad. He had outgrown the valley's twelve- to fourteen-inch trout and the rivers. He needed to find bigger water and bigger fish. He settled in Helena, Montana, about two years ago, and between shifts at his day job, he started working for a fly shop in Craig. He bought a drift boat and now can speak fluently about the makes and models of fly rods at every price point. He knows the Latin names of whatever is hatching and how to best imitate that bug.

Now Brad combs over the mighty Missouri. The chances that he's fishing the river right now are higher than they should be.

So far, Chadd and I have made the trip up to fish with Brad once. We aimed for an early fall trip but didn't make it there until early November. We came the same week as winter. We shivered and threw sloppy casts with flies too big for our rods. Brad took us right to the dam, and we fished down. All of us eventually caught some of those slow, determined rainbows, but it was harder than it should have been.

Leaning against some bankside rocks, trying to beat feeling back into our fingers, we watched a family of deer swim from one side of the river to the other only to turn around a few minutes later and swim right back with just their heads jutting out of the water.

Brad shook his head. "They do this all day. Just go back and forth and back again. I don't get it. It's like they just want to get wet or something."

Any river occasionally obscures everything but itself—maybe out of self-preservation, or maybe it's something less romantic.

We watched as the deer exited the water and shook like dogs.

From the banks of the Missouri, we saw men outfitted with the most expensive gear jaded at catching another three-pound trout. And we saw people in johnboats throwing mealworms and not stopping at their limits. Brad fits into neither of these groups.

I hope the Missouri appreciates what it has in Brad as an angler: someone who will respect the river; someone who will dig in and protect the river; someone who will find out what's best for it and enact change to keep it as it is and maybe even make it better; someone who will tell stories but not lies about it.

But of course, the Missouri doesn't care because it can't. It only moves its water, fish, sediment and Brad's drift boat down, always slowly down.

Because Brad's family still lives in northern Utah, I see him a few times a year. Last time, Brad, Chadd and I made an effort to fish together. We got in the car and did the normal things. We asked about one another's families and jobs. We asked how the fishing had been. Brad told us he had "figured out" streamer fishing and spey casting. And I don't doubt it. He also said that he and Janelle had figured it out; she even comes and rows the boat for him, and they're happy.

We drove to the Cub River, maybe fifteen miles from where we first fished together. The sky was dark gray. It wasn't really raining as much as just being wet. Despite the gloomy sky, it was warm, and bugs moved on the water but nothing spectacular. The small stream is perfect for tenkara rods, which is what we all fished that day. Brad had his video camera and seemed much more interested in taking footage than catching fish. He no longer jogged to the river while we geared up like he had done when he lived in the valley.

Instead, Brad had slowed down. He watched us both cast. Eventually, he said, "This is a special river. One of a kind. And you guys have it dialed in."

It was flattering, but Chadd and I didn't respond. We knew Brad could outfish us even though we were fishing a stretch he had never seen before. But Brad didn't fish much at all that day. Instead, he took long pulls from his water bottle. When we'd fail to pass our flies over a certain section, he'd lazily point and say, "That spot's not done yet." He fished only when he veered from Chadd and me. And always (always) caught a fish within minutes of

It's as if the slow-moving Missouri had steeped him.

wetting his line. He was still excited but no longer desperate. It's as if the slow-moving Missouri had steeped him.

When the sky grew darker, we scaled a rock face to get out of the river. A finger of rock extended out like a peninsula. A blanket of fall had spread on the canyon, and river nearly circled us thirty feet below.

"Wait, guys. Let's get a picture." Chadd set his camera on a rock. He aimed it so you can see the river snaking below us, but eventually, the canyon swallows it. Chadd looks cheeky, I look stoic and Brad, well, Brad just looks happy. He's stripped of adult pretension and is just there waiting for the canyon to swallow him like that river.

THEN CAME NOVEMBER

Chadd VanZanten

Let me explain the way winter arrives here at the northern tip of the Wasatch Front. You might be under the impression it arrives at the winter solstice, December 21, or thereabouts, the same as in other places. You might think it has something to do with the declination of the sun—the way it rides so low in the sky and sets before ever chasing the icy sparkle from the banked-up snow.

You'd be wrong.

Around here, winter begins in December, but it arrives much earlier. It may come as early as Labor Day. It might hold off until Thanksgiving. Most typically, it's October.

It happens like this. You hike up a hollow in Blacksmith Fork Canyon to fly-fish an isolated stretch of that river. The maple leaves are blood red and the aspens are golden, but at noon, you'd swear it's still August. So, you're wearing a T-shirt. There are nine different flies pinned to your cap, but you've not decided which to tie on yet because the fish you're after haven't exhibited the faintest sign of choosiness for several months. They'll bite down on almost anything.

Then you notice the grasshoppers fleeing through the dry grass at your feet, and just as you're about to bring this to the attention of your fishing buddy, a wet gray cloud slides across the sun, and instead, you ask him, "Hey, did you bring a jacket?"

"No," he says, face upturned. "Did you?"

"I didn't."

It gets cold in a hurry, but you fish anyway. The wind blows, and there's rain. Hands get so raw and pruned you start trying to remember where you left your winter gloves—somewhere in your truck, hopefully. You catch fewer fish than you caught a week ago. Fewer by half. That's because you're fishing as if it's summer. But it's not. Winter has arrived. It hasn't started yet, but it has come.

This year, winter hit me like a delivery van. The last thing I remember distinctly is a trip to the outer Cub River in mid-October. The water was clear as gin, and a rust-colored caddis fly worked all day like a voodoo fetish to coax almost fifty cutthroat trout to my net.

Those cutthroats were reckless. They came up from deep holes, crossed from one side of the channel to the other to take a fly. They came up two at a time. Those fish were irrational. I was extra careful when returning each to the stream that day. Clearly, they could not be trusted with their own safety.

After the sun ducked behind the limestone rim of the canyon, the fishing cooled off. I sat down to remove a pebble from my boot. I had been walking on it for hours, thinking if I stopped even for a minute to take it out, I might break the spell. That was the last in a string of such days.

Then came November, and there he was: winter. Unmistakable.

A temperature inversion—a mass of frigid, immovable air—settled into the valley, trapping beneath it a dirty mist of ice and automobile exhaust. The sun shone whitely through the haze like a portal to some paler, colder universe.

For a week solid, it never got above twenty degrees. The fog grew so dense that the Wellsville Mountains, which rise like a fortress wall at the western edge of the valley, were obscured from view for days, glimpsed only at evening against the violet pollution of sundown.

Anchor ice began appearing on the floor of the Logan River. The small tributary streams like Rock Creek and Right Hand Fork were already frozen over. The city workers got out the fire hoses at night and started laying down the ice-skating rink, a ritual that typically doesn't commence until after the holidays are completely done.

It wasn't even December yet.

When the days grow short and dim, everything seems more serious than it actually is. A summertime problem is a wintertime crisis. A crisis in autumn becomes a calamity just a month or two later. If I tell you I was struggling with a major personal emergency in early November, that should indicate my condition on the first weekend in December, which is when it got even colder. Single-digit temperatures during the day and below zero all night.

Such extremes are not unknown here. There is a place in Logan Canyon where the temperature may dip to sixty degrees below zero. But that's only in the dead cold of January and at an elevation of 8,100 feet. I was wallowing down in the valley floor, and the winter solstice was still two weeks away.

Ordinarily, I wouldn't fish in weather like that, and my autumn crisis made me want to fish even less. But I'd made arrangements to fish with my friend Littrell, who was visiting from Texas. Littrell had never fished this part of the country, and although he was here on business and staying for only a few days, he'd gotten it into his head that he must catch a trout from one of our high mountain streams.

I advised against this.

"You understand how cold it is out there," I said.

"Yes."

"You understand there's a decent chance we may perish," I said.

"I'd still like to give it a try."

On the morning of December 7, the temperature stood at five degrees. The inversion was gone, but the wind gusted to twenty knots. Factoring wind chill, it was seventeen below zero at the Spring Hollow bridge, which is where we stepped lightly over the bankside shelves of ice and lowered ourselves into the Logan River.

We fished. I number that day among the worst I've ever known. After each cast, the water froze onto the actual fly line, forming a glassy chain that could be cleared off only with considerable effort. It's a phenomenon I'd never experienced. Between that and the down-canyon wind, it was difficult even to cast in a forward direction, and accuracy was out of the question. My waders, too, were laminated in ice, and hoarfrost formed on my beard.

After twenty minutes, Littrell shouted, "I can't cast. Everything's frozen up."

I shouldered my rod and slogged across the stream to him. Windblown spray stung my face and froze on my glasses. I steered Littrell toward the one promising river bend I thought we might prospect before succumbing to exposure.

"Cast in there," I said, pointing, voice raised against the wind. "Cast right in there."

Littrell's ice-hampered fly line flopped over heavily and nowhere in the vicinity I'd indicated.

"There?" he asked.

"If that is the best you can do, then, yes. There."

By some accident, Littrell's fly slid through the bend, and he set his hook on a small brown trout. I took a photograph as evidence that it had happened. It was hard to know if that fish even wanted to get back in the water. Within ten minutes, we had retreated to our trucks, and we have not spoken of the matter since.

It was hard to know if that fish even wanted to get back in the water.

My troubles worsened. I lost track of what day it was, forgot appointments. I slept a lot. My family asked me what was wrong. I refused to explain myself. Friends told me they were worried. I claimed to be fine. My plan was to fish through it all, to take my problems into the mountains and lay them there like some melancholy and reticent hero. This didn't really work. Winter had pushed me to the ground, and I guess he stood with his foot on my neck awhile because I couldn't take a clean, deep breath for a month.

But there's something else that happens in wintertime around here. Every so often, there is a break in the weather. Despite my many years in the valley, I'd forgotten.

It happens like this. You go out to your truck carrying your fly rod and net, and although the garage is a mere thirty feet from the back door, you put on gloves and wrap a scarf over your face to prevent your nostrils from freezing shut. As you drive, you hold one hand over the heater vent, then the other, wondering if you might reach the Blacksmith Fork before the truck even warms up.

Then you notice a rupture in the canopy of the inversion, out over the Wellsvilles, as if there were a weak spot in the sky there. You fumble for your sunglasses as the sun glares through the gloom. Soon the haze overhead turns dark blue and all around is melting, dripping.

This year the break came when I met up one day to fish with Jason at the Oneida Narrows on the Bear River. It lies at the uppermost limits of the Wasatch, on the Idaho side. Jason brought his dog, a yellow lab that waits by the riverbank while we fish, then charges madly into the water to chase the fish we hook.

We call her the Blonde Torpedo of Destiny.

It was the first time in a long time I'd fished the Bear. As we drove along the back roads through the old township site of Egypt and north through the pasturelands, I confessed I didn't know the best way to catch anything that day.

"We can swing some streamers," said Jason.

"Maybe try some nymphs," I replied.

When we stepped out of Jason's mud-sprayed Honda, we knew it was the kind of day when catching fish is less than paramount. The air was clear and windless, the sky an improbable cerulean.

It got warmer as we pulled on our waders and hiked a mile or so downstream. Everything was melting, dripping. The Blonde Torpedo loped out ahead through the snow, mouth agape, tongue lolling. A bald eagle coursed overhead so low I saw its eye winking like a camera shutter as it tilted its head to examine us.

We swung our streamers. We tried some nymphs. The fish obliged us.

I watched Jason hook a small rainbow trout. His dog splashed over to investigate as the fish was landed and let go again. I squinted into the glimmer of the sun on the water. Jason raised his face to the sky.

"This day," he said, shaking the water from his hand. "I mean, my God, what a day."

The vernal equinox would fall on the twentieth of March, then and always, here and everywhere. But in Cache Valley, spring had arrived. It hadn't started, but it had come.

Rule 2

FISH WHERE YOU'RE AT

A Good Place to Make Saints

Russ Beck

*The wilderness and the solitary place shall be glad for them;
and the desert shall rejoice, and blossom as the rose.*
—Isaiah 35:1

I imagine it started with a single shovel load. Simon T. Beck threw some rich, brown mountain earth into Reeder Creek and watched it disperse. He threw in a few more loads. He moved some rocks and diverted the stream a couple of feet. Then he got his son, my granddad Osmer, to help him.

Simon may never have moved the stream if it wasn't for Brigham Young. When he entered the Salt Lake Valley, he slammed his cane into the dry ground and declared, "Right here will stand the temple of our God." That same week, Young's followers started to survey and build up a city from the desert floor. At what would be the city's center, they laid the foundation for a temple.

When pressured by others to push ahead to California, where the ground was wet and the soil fertile, Young replied, "This is a good place to make saints."

Young would die forty years later, but in that time, he would organize and establish 350 colonies, mostly in Utah and southern Idaho but some as far away as Mexico and Canada. His goal was a God-centered, self-sustaining, utopian society.

Then he got his son, my granddad Osmer, to help him.

One of Young's settlements in central Utah, Little Denmark (now Spring City), stumbles at the base of two mountains. The pioneers called the larger one "God's Armchair" and the slightly smaller one "Bishop's Armchair." Apart from a few veins of rich earth that a creek dragged down from the mountains, Spring City's soil was acrid and white with oolitic sediment. Half a dozen natural springs dotted the valley, but they were hotly contended by the local Blackhawks who regularly raided the Mormon settlers. One homesteader said of the valley, "Not even a jackrabbit could exist." The only things that seemed to thrive were sagebrush and rattlesnakes.

Spring City finally turned a corner around 1900. In February 1913, twenty thousand jackrabbits—the same rabbits that people thought couldn't survive—were captured in and around the town. Everybody and everything—except the Blackhawks and the jackrabbits—seemed to enjoy some ease.

But Spring City reached its capacity. There wasn't enough arable soil to sustain a larger population, and only so many people could work at the local café, general store, creamery, saloon and milling company. They believed they were commanded by prophets and God to make the land yield support

Streams now connect a collection of dammed reservoirs, and the land drips with cow cabbage and cheat grass.

for their growing population, and when the most God could offer was a rainstorm here and a mild winter there, the settlers endeavored to change the one thing that would actually sustain them: the land itself, down to the character of the soil.

The mountain I knew growing up is different from the one my great-grandfather Simon T. Beck knew—and partly because of him. Streams now connect a collection of dammed reservoirs, and the land drips with cow cabbage and cheat grass. The mountain, covered in thick pines (now tinder because of beetles) and aspens, had elk and deer sleeping in the shade.

I learned to fish—really fish—up there on an outlet to Gooseberry reservoir. The stream, almost all undercut banks, has some sections nearly going underground.

Kirk Benge—a kid eager to piss off something in nature who would grow up to be a man with a pet monkey named Gonorrhea and a job with the Utah State Health Lab, where he gets heads of dogs, cougars, cats, squirrels and raccoons regularly mailed to him—taught me to fish there when we were in high school. I started on the lakes and reservoirs with my dad and the Boy Scouts, but that fishing always felt predicated on something other than skill or work. Instead, it was an equation almost completely dependent on time spent at the lip of a lake.

Kirk taught me to comb over the cheat grass and find a neon-green grasshopper. We'd pierce their bodies with our small golden Eagle Claw hooks. Something resembling runny peanut butter would ooze out and stick to our fingers. We'd look in the shadows of the undercut banks for those errant rainbow trout, rebel fish that had snuck past the cement outlet, threaded the gate and found a wild home away from the controlled reservoir. They were stupid for our hoppers. We'd toss out the mess of guts and limbs, and they'd hit hard.

That small outlet is the first place I ever had a double-digit day. That was the first time I felt euphoric about fishing—maybe the first time I felt euphoric about anything.

About fifteen miles south of where Gooseberry is now, Simon T. Beck ran sheep in the shadow of God's Armchair. When he tired of eating beef and mutton, he fished for cutthroats in the small streams that wound on top of the flat mountain. He didn't need rods, lures, flies or bait. He'd lean over a fallen log crossing the stream and drop a naked hook in the water, and the fish would strike. He noticed most of the water eventually sloped off the east side of the mountain, away from Spring City. That's when he got the idea to move the water.

He didn't need rods, lures, flies or bait. He'd lean over a fallen log crossing the stream and drop a naked hook in the water, and the fish would strike.

After Simon and Osmer bent Reeder Creek for a few summers, they talked to others and got help. The stream that once left the mountain to the east now flows west. It's the same waterway that threads my family's land to include my childhood home's backyard. My mom told me not to, but I would spend hours balancing on the rocks trying not to get my sneakers wet. Cockleburs would cover me and whichever dog I had with me, and my shoes had enough soil caked on them to start a medium-sized herb garden.

Nearly a decade after Simon died, the town received New Deal money, and Civilian Conservation Corps workers burrowed through the mountain (twice) to bring more water and soil down to the valley. They built dams and made valleys into lakes. In the 1960s, they chopped terraces into the mountain to sponge up more water.

I never met my granddad or great-granddad—they both passed before I was born—but as much as nearly anybody, they're responsible for showing me the water and the trout on top of that mountain that changed me into an angler.

I've taken an ATV down a trail where Reeder Creek once ran but only once. It's now a maze of pine stands and deadfall. It's puckered, wilted and brittle.

In the Fortress of the Sandhill Crane

Chadd VanZanten

I took Russ Beck fishing on Rock Creek because I'd been there and he hadn't and I knew once we got up there, he'd say, "Good grief."

That's what Russ Beck says when he thinks something is really impressive.

Like the time we drove to Montana to fish the Missouri River with our friend Brad. It was an eight-hour drive. Montana really is one of our larger states. It's number four. After driving for three hours, we ran out of things to say, but we kept on talking for another couple hours just to be sure, I guess. Then Russ told me to find some music, so I played some Joy Division.

"Good grief," he said. He turned up the volume. "This is so good."

We made it to Brad's house in Helena. Brad and Janelle let us stay with them and fed us homemade pizza. We sat on their living room floor watching TV and tying flies and eating slice after slice of the pizza.

"Good grief, you guys," said Russ. "This is awesome. Thank you."

When Russ Beck farts, he just tells you. He's not embarrassed about it. I guess he doesn't want anyone to wonder who did it. So he just announces it. He was crossing the living room to get more pizza when he farted.

"I farted," he said.

Everybody laughed. Janelle had a mouthful of food, and she was laughing so hard her eyes filled up with tears. Eventually, she tipped over sideways because she couldn't breathe properly.

To reach Rock Creek, you drive up the highway for a while and then get on a gravel road, followed by a jeep trail. After that, you walk for a while through a stone-strewn dell, threading your way between clumps of sage and juniper brakes. It was spring, and the ruddy bankside willows were sending their new shoots skyward like CB antennas.

The first part of the stream is a series of meanders, five or six bend pools in a row, all alike and each with at least one trout waiting, sometimes two. It's premium tenkara country. The fish don't grow to immense size in Rock Creek, but every so often, you hook a big one, which makes you think more highly of smaller ones. We caught some fish. They were mostly cutthroats.

"Good grief," said Russ. "This is gorgeous up here."

This was back when Brad had just finished his master's thesis. I proofread the whole thing for him. Didn't charge him a dime. There was no way I could—he didn't have any money. But even if he did, I wouldn't have. It was that good.

It was all about how the West has changed according to who was in charge at the time. First, the Native Americans, then European settlers and now us. His goal was not to lay blame. It wasn't an indictment. It was a record of the stories.

There were stories of how the Bear River drainage was once so choked with cutthroat trout the Shoshone could simply pick them up and walk away. It's one of the reasons they settled along its banks. Then came the lumberjacks and sawmills—and then the sheep and cattle.

And there's the story of a bunch of Mormons who tried to plant eels and lobsters and oysters in the Great Salt Lake. I can't help but cringe at the idea of any aquatic lifeform dropped into that hot, briny soup. Surely an oyster would be happier in a lake of battery acid. But they did it. They'd bring over barrels of live fish from California on trains. Carp and bass. Salmon! They were planting fish the way you might plant a peach pit or sunflower seeds or eggplant starts in your backyard just to see if they'll grow. For the fish-planting Mormons, the answer was usually "no."

But deforestation and exotic species introductions aren't the only ways the West changed. Brad said it doesn't matter who or where you are. You can't live in

Brad said it doesn't matter who or where you are. You can't live in a place without changing it. The Indians couldn't, and neither can we.

a place without changing it. The Indians couldn't, and neither can we. He also said there was no one perfect state of nature, that humans didn't just stumble along and foul up some unspoiled and static Eden that had existed for uncounted millennia. Nature changes herself all the time, even when people aren't around.

Keeping records of the changes—that's where Brad's interests lay. Curating what was here when we showed up and documenting what happened next makes us mindful of the changes we make. Documentation makes us accountable, too, and more thoughtful. Smarter, maybe. Hopefully.

"Brad said in his thesis this whole mountain used to be covered in pine timber." I said that to Russ, out there on Rock Creek. "Not sagebrush and juniper like now. All timber."

"Can you imagine this place as just one big forest?" said Russ, scanning the scrub-dotted hills.

"Yeah, I know."

"Good grief."

The next part of Rock Creek is a beaver dam complex, a spread-out pond with dead willow branches sticking up and bleaching in the sun. The

I became all at once aware of my own immense presence there in the stream, and it felt a lot like embarrassment.

untroubled face of the water reflected the unblemished and limitless blue above. At first, we skirted the margins of the pond, casting into the center, but it was hard fishing that way. The fish were always just out of reach. So we waded in, stalking through a forest of bones.

A fish rose beneath the arching limbs of an enormous and deceased willow tree. Then he rose again. There was no way I could ever cast to him. There were too many branches guarding the way. But I turned and went over there anyway just to be sure, I guess. The water was up to my waist. I waded slowly so the fish wouldn't startle. Plumes of mud boiled up behind me.

As I approached the big dead willow, a sandhill crane rose up and spread her wings. With one great wing beat, she was airborne, so close I felt the wind of it on my face. At first, I thought the crane was going to pounce on me and drive me down into the muddy water. She probably could have. They're definitely one of our larger birds. But instead, she hung motionless for a split second in the air, brilliant in the sunlight against the empty blue sky, and then wheeled to one side and flew away.

The crane had been sitting a nest down in the base of the big willow, whose branches were the pickets and battlements of its fortress. The beaver dam was her moat.

I could have investigated the mound of the nest. It was right there. I could have gone over and peeked at the eggs or young. But I became all at once aware of my own immense presence there in the stream, and it felt a lot like embarrassment. To have jumped the crane that way, to have blundered into her battlements. And so I backed up and turned around and got out of the beaver dam. My boots and waders were black and slick with mud.

As we hiked downstream and back to the truck, we heard the sandhill crane's agitated chattering. She was up on a hillside behind us. She bobbed through the juniper trees and watched us, peculiar and yet graceful, waiting for us to clear out.

AMERICA'S CAVEAT RIVER

Russ Beck

I grew up in a town that had a story for nearly every run-down property in its borders. Most buildings had at least one ghost floating around its fence line, but the really haunted estate—the one where, supposedly, my

I choose to fish those tributaries that feed the river instead of the convenient pullouts where the Bear threads the road. I'm always looking for the less obvious place to fish because everyone knows the story goes that you have to work for the big fish.

great-great-uncle plastered babies into the walls, where it's said he threw his wife into the well, where the land itself swallows livestock and spits out bones, where you can still hear screams coiling up near the hawthorn bushes and willow trees—is just outside town. It's just far enough to escape the reach of the city lights but not so far that you won't make it back by morning. The location, more than its history, is probably the reason for the stories. If there is no journey, there is no room for stories to germinate.

My friend Dr. Lynne S. McNeil is a folklorist. She told me that it's common for haunted things to happen in liminal spaces, the places between places. So the haunted house on the edge of town makes sense, as does the fact that most of the people who went to the haunted house were teenagers—not yet adults but not kids either. It's human to seek out nooks to create the things we fear and the things we feel compelled to lie about. She also told me about the theory of ostension. People act out something of the legend to connect to the legend more. It's not enough just to go to the haunted house, but you have to throw stones in the well to see if the motion of something falling will waken the long-murdered wife.

I now live near the geographic center of the Bear River drainage. I can walk to decent water from my house. But I hardly ever fish it, mostly because the best fishing in northern Utah is in southern Idaho. Some of it is right on the border. There's something in the trip. It's more of an event if the trip distance is increased even by fifteen minutes. The Bear River travels nearly five hundred miles, but its mouth and source are separated by only about one hundred. It starts and ends in Utah but crosses the borders of five states. It's the largest river in North America that doesn't flow to an ocean. It is known for its calm meanderings and its white-water kayak sections. It is America's caveat river. Almost as an homage to the river that always needs an explanation, I choose to travel to it. I choose to fish those tributaries that feed the river instead of the convenient pullouts where the Bear threads the road. I like to follow the fish to where they spawn. I'm always looking for the less obvious place to fish because everyone knows the story goes that you have to work for the big fish. Fishing trips need time to steep both before and after fishing, time when, if you fish with others, they'll tell you how the fishing is going to be or was that day or, if you fish alone, you'll think about how the fishing will actually be or was that day. You'll compare it to other times at the same place, and you'll remember both real and imaginary fish. If there isn't a space between fishing and not fishing to think and create, if you don't drive past water that looks fine in search of great water, the fishing won't be as good. I'll never be a guy who spends more time on the road consistently than in the river, but I'll always give the fish and the river the respect of a drive.

Rule 3

FISH WHERE YOU END UP

THE PLACES WE END UP AT

Chadd VanZanten

Brad calls the motel around 8:00 p.m. to tell them we're on the interstate and about two hours away, but will there be someone to check us in when we arrive?

I should mention my use of the word "motel" in this case is generous. We're heading to a cluster of shoddy cabins out back of an old roadside stopover. It doesn't matter whether it was originally a gas station that became a gift shop or a diner that became a convenience store because it is now all of those things and the one thing it is not is a motel.

All-night check-in is just one of the many conveniences they do not boast. Air conditioning, ice and room service are a few others, and we are surely closer to the Continental Divide than the nearest swimming pool or hot tub. They have no Wi-Fi. For all I know, they are still awaiting the arrival of hi-fi.

The proprietress of this establishment tells Brad the diner closes at 10:00 p.m. Her name is Brandy. She says if we get there before then, someone can give us a key to our cabin. If we get there after, we can "go around back" and find the key under or next to something somewhere, but that seems worrisomely complicated. So Paul drives a little faster.

We exit the interstate and pull into the gravel parking lot with about 120 seconds to spare but no more than that. Through the windows of the diner, we see Brandy closing up. She wears way too much makeup and spray-on tan for someone her age, and her attempt to flirt with Russ would be awkward even if she were much younger. However, she wins us over by treating us not as paying customers but as distant and unexpected in-laws who are in need of a place to crash.

"So," she says, "you're here."

We admit that we are.

She asks if we want to pay with cash or check, and in return, we ask her if she can split our bill four ways so that we can each pay separately.

"Well," she says, "that makes it harder for me."

No one says anything for a few moments.

"So, canya or can'tcha?" says Paul.

"Yeah, I can."

As she runs our cards, we ask her how business has been. She sighs and says her best employee is out of commission tonight because she had to go into town to bail her boyfriend out of jail.

We nod and pretend to know how tough it is when your best employee has to go into town to bail her boyfriend out of jail. Brandy shrugs it off and says everything will be fine in the morning.

"I mean, how long do you need to bail one guy out of jail, right?"

We nod some more.

Brandy shows us to our cabin, the interior of which would not be unfamiliar to anyone who has been detained in an internment camp. Once we've dropped our bags and rod cases, we notice the cabin has only three beds, so Brandy takes us to the cabin next door, where she keeps a couple rollaway cots that appear to have been in service since the Roosevelt administration, and I mean Teddy. She points out which is the better of the pair, and Russ helps me roll it down the boardwalk to our cabin.

Brandy watches Russ as he pushes the rollaway. "You're tall," she says. "How tall are you?"

Once inside the room, I unfold the cot, and there in the center of the mattress is an evil-colored stain about the diameter of a good-sized dinner plate.

Russ and I exchange a horrified glance, but Brandy is unfazed. I realize that it falls to me to be embarrassed on behalf of us all, and so I quickly flip the mattress over.

On the other side the stain is even larger.

"Try again," says Russ.

I turn the mattress back over and say, "We're sure this is the best one?"

Our cabin, the interior of which would not be unfamiliar to anyone who has been detained in an internment camp.

"Yeah," says Brandy, wrinkling her nose. "The other one has mice living in it."

These are the places where we end up when we decide it's time for a fishing trip: at the convenience store that sells car batteries, handmade costume jewelry and expired Tylenol side by side on the same shelf or at the filling station that makes the best fried chicken in the entire region but has a restroom so foul you'd use it only in cases of great emergency.

Greasy places. Smelly places. But open places, too.

Brandy brings some bedding and linen. I use both sheets to double wrap the mattress like a corpse. As soon as I lie down, I pretty much know how sore I'll be in the morning. This mattress will hit me in my lower back and hips because it sags in the middle exactly like a hammock, and there are good reasons one does not see many hammocks in the bedrooms of Western civilization.

This is one of the few advantages of very Spartan travel accommodations: you at least know how much worse it can get and you're unsurprised when it does.

We did most of our talking in the truck, so we flip off the lights and turn in. Outside in the parking lot, idling big-rigs growl ceaselessly through the night. A sodium-arc lamp on a high mast floods the cabin with ruddy electric moonlight. Clouds of big moths swarm in the glare, and occasionally, they land on the window, where they dance in circles and figure-eight patterns.

The next morning, we're up and in the stream before the sun gets there. We catch a few fish—I hook and lose a nice brown trout practically on my first cast. However, as the day advances, there seems to be a discrepancy. I came on this trip for the superb fishing, and the fishing is not superb. My attitude deteriorates, and that makes me fish poorly, which makes me catch even less.

"They're in here," says Brad. He's hammering away at the deeper water with his nymphs. "You know they're in here. We just have to figure it out."

I hate it when Brad says that because that's what Brad says when the fishing sucks. And you can't pretend you don't mind. As soon as you tell yourself it's not about the fish, that's when you know the fish are exactly what it's about. This is another place where we end up—somewhere the fishing ought to be good but is not, and the river offers no explanation.

As the day grows hot, the fishing worsens, though that seems hardly possible. Russ and I fish a brushy, technical stretch of stream breathtaking for the massive potential of its shady pocket water and plunge pools, but we catch nothing. Brad and Paul's afternoon is much the same, so we take a break and eat some lunch. Paul drives us around the countryside to reconnoiter various other waterways, and we even stop to visit with some landowners for local intel. I fall asleep in the truck a couple times.

Evening comes, and it cools off. We return to the stream and split up to refish various sections that performed poorly in the heat of the day. I've given up hope of a fifty-fish day or even a twenty-fish day. I go up the road a mile or so to a slow, deep bend in the stream where we'd caught a few nice fish that morning.

As I approach the river and find a good spot to begin, I see animals moving in the high grass at the bank. It's a herd of twenty or more big-horn sheep. They emerge from the grass and pass within fifty feet of me before climbing a rocky hillside. It's juveniles and ewes, with horns that don't curl all the way around. Their orderly but slightly nervous procession reminds me of a grade school class during a fire drill. Sixty seconds later, they've climbed over the hill and out of sight.

I walk to the spot and stand there in the laid-over grass where the little herd had been resting and drinking. They've left behind a faint, animal odor. As I survey the water for rising fish (there are none), it occurs to me that all around me is silence, and I mean silence. No breeze or birdsong. The low-

It's a rare and utterly welcome sensation, and it's where I wanted to end up all along.

gradient stream makes no sound, and there are no trucks moving along the dirt road. It stays this way for a long time. It's a rare and utterly welcome sensation, and it's where I wanted to end up all along.

AMERICAN AND CANADIAN FOOTBALL

Russ Beck

My dad and the doctor who delivered me are still friends. The doctor is retired now, and he lives in a house perched on a bench that overlooks the valley where I grew up. From his house, I can see my elementary school, my middle school and my high school. If I look south, I can almost see the school where I started college. There isn't much in this desert valley, but what water is there twinkles and shimmers. It's almost as though it shakes. The towns are like splotches of bacteria colonies in a petri dish while the fields of grain and alfalfa checkerboard the flat areas.

Legend has it that the neighboring mountain range is a sleeping woman, and from my doctor's house, it sure looks like the legends are true.

He also has a small pond filled with trout.

I didn't go for the view.

As we drove to the pond, my dad said, "You'll be surprised when you see them."

"Well, if we catch anything."

He chuckled. "You'll catch something."

I'm weary of sure things—especially in fishing. Promises build expectations that can rarely be met. I would rather fish somewhere that I've heard nothing about and slowly write my own ideas of the water.

He fought my light 4-weight, but eventually, I pulled him in, a mature tiger trout with a hooked jaw and a humped back.

On the east side, a spring fed the pond. Cattails and cottonwoods bordered it on the west. Damsel flies mated everywhere, but nothing else was in the air. The pond surface rippled because of meaty backs breaking and splashing. The takes looked more like an athletic event than feeding fish.

I tied on the first fly I found in my box, which was a Turk's Tarantula. I went over to where the spring fed the pond and tossed in a warm-up cast.

Instantly, something big took the fly.

He fought my light 4-weight, but eventually, I pulled him in, a mature tiger trout with a hooked jaw and a humped back.

This was the pattern. I tossed out a fly, wiggled it occasionally and waited for the hit. Nearly every cast produced a fish, and not just fish but bigger fish than I ever catch on my home waters.

Eventually, I started to expected fish instead of trying to earn them. I stopped playing the fish and just started pulling them in, which resulted in a broken tippet. But I didn't lament the break because I knew it wasn't a lost fish but a delayed fish. When I lost my Turk's, I threw on a salmon fly imitation, knowing full well that I was miles (if not a hundred miles) from the nearest salmon fly hatch. I continued to pull in fish until an eager tiger broke my line right at the shore. I changed to a Woolly Bugger. The clear water allowed me to watch it sink, slowly undulating to the bottom. Before I could retrieve any line, a school swarmed. Something took the bugger. The fish's silver head shot out of the water and broke my 4x tippet without much effort. No longer connected to my line, it surfaced again just to show me what I missed. This time he cleared the water. He was a rainbow that looked like a fat kid belly flopping in a public pool.

Soon I felt guilty. I didn't have the right equipment for this pond. My rod was too small to bring these fish in quickly so they wouldn't wear out. And all those trout with my flies hanging off their lips like cigarettes they couldn't spit out—all because I didn't have sufficiently heavy tippet.

But I kept on fishing much longer than I should have. Eventually, my wife wandered over and asked if she could give it a try. She threw out a pile of line, and the fish still jumbled to take her fly. She slowly pulled in probably the biggest fish of the day, a rainbow whose colors were nearly nonexistent.

It was fishing, I guess. Like Canadian football is technically football. But something is missed by pulling up to the lip of a pond and instantly catching fish.

Last summer, I fished a stretch of very familiar water on a day when it had rained. I could feel the canyon shrink as the stream swelled. I found the rock that shunts the stream south and just leaned into the current and watched. I knew I would catch a fish in that hole because I always caught a fish in that

When I cast into the sweeping current, something unexpected happened—nothing.

hole. It was guaranteed. The expectation was exactly the same as what I felt at the pond.

When I cast into the sweeping current, something unexpected happened—nothing.

I watched my fly drift down untouched. Then I tried again, and the same thing happened. I felt tension rise beneath my soaked T-shirt, and I let it stay there. And when I caught a fish where I didn't expect to three yards away from the guarantee hole, I felt that tension dissolve.

The pond offered no tension, and as every good angler knows, tension is the key to good fishing, be it knots, lines or missed fish.

Would I go to the pond again? Yes. I'd go right now. But it's not the same, and I think it would get old.

As we drove back to the house, my dad asked, "So, what do you think?"

"It was fun. The fish were huge."

"You didn't even see one of the big ones."

"You've seen bigger in the pond?"

He chuckled again, "I've caught bigger in the pond."

TERRESTRIALS ADRIFT

Chadd VanZanten

In rivers, the water you touch is the last of what has passed and the first of that which is to come; so with present time.
—*Leonardo da Vinci*

It gets late before we finally make a decision. We settle on the Canyon Section of the Snake River, just upstream from Palisades Reservoir and downstream from iconic white-water rapids like Big Kahuna and the Lunch Counter.

Ken's got a big USGS map spread over his kitchen table. He taps a spot where the heavy black line of the highway meets the blue serpentine of the river.

"We get in here," he says. Then he traces the river with his finger. It takes a couple seconds. "Get out here."

Ken seems to be in favor of some shorter section. He tells us the Canyon Section is twenty-five miles long and that it will take all day to fish and then some. But that's what we want, I argue—an all-day gig.

"What we don't want to do is run out of water," I reason. "If we float the long section, we might run out of daylight, but we won't run out of river."

"I'll go anywhere," says Russ.

"I'm bringing a headlamp," says Ken, folding up the map.

It's a little after 8:00 a.m. when we get to the put-in. A river guide is putting in his drift boat ahead of us. He's got two old guys as paying customers. The short one has a white, pencil-thin mustache and a rumpled ball cap. The tall one wears enormous sunglasses and an old-fashioned fishing hat. He talks continuously, cracking wise with us, while we wait.

"Jeeze," he says, "would you look at all the food these guys packed?" He points at our provisions and elbows his buddy. "Chips, jerky, lemonade, fruit? How long you gonna be gone?"

Well. That's the question.

I've never fished the Snake before, so I try to take a peek at what flies the two old guys have on their lines. But they hold their rods with their hands over the hook keepers, as if hiding them.

"So, what's the fly of the day?" I ask.

They look to their guide, who gives them a quick head shake. The guy in the old fishing hat shrugs and keeps talking as he clambers into the boat. He wishes us good luck, and we hear him prattle on as they drift out of earshot.

"So, what's the fly of the day?" I ask.

Now and then, we anchor up on vast gravel bars, where we snack and wet-wade.

The day proceeds clear and warm, and there is almost no wind. As we slide downstream, towering cottonwoods and jutting formations of black basalt loom against the blue sky. With our 6-weights, we cast big terrestrials close into the banks, where there are rainbows, browns and cutthroats waiting beneath the overhanging grass and branches. Now and then, we anchor up on vast gravel bars, where we snack and wet-wade.

Ken rows most of the time, but Russ and I take a couple turns, too. Two blisters develop on my right hand, one from casting and one from rowing, meaning I have a lot to learn about both pursuits.

Ken tries to coach us and fish at the same time. He's more successful at the former than the latter.

"Point the nose of the boat where you don't want to go," he tells us. "Aim the stern to where you do want to go. Then, just pull the oars and let the river do the rest."

He teaches us about pillows, sweepers and standing waves. He explains how some currents push you away while others pull you in.

We alternate our positions in the boat: Russ in front, then Ken and then me. The river goes on and on.

"I have a blister, and my blister has a blister," says Russ, picking at his palm.

At last, we near the end of the Canyon Section. The sun drops from view, and the river lies in blue shade. In my memory, that day stretches out behind me like the shadow of a fencepost at sundown—elongated, nearly endless.

I'm still on the oars at the very end, and I think I'm sort of getting the hang of it. But then I almost miss the entrance to the takeout. When I finally get us paddled in, I just about clunk into another fellow's drift boat, which would be only slightly less insulting than feeling up his wife.

Ken kibitzes patiently at me until I somehow collide with the floating dock at the take-out. Even then, I bring us in at a weird angle, and when Ken jumps out, he barks his shin on the gunwale. We help Ken trailer up his boat, and we all get in the truck.

"That was awesome," says Russ. "Now. Where is the nearest steakhouse?"

In the dark, we drive to a bar where the river guides hang out. The parking lot is full of trucks and drift boats and not much else. We joke about how many fights have likely gone down there.

"Technically, I don't think we're done here until one of us gets a couple teeth knocked out," I say.

Inside, the place is rowdy with grizzled, dark-tanned guys in ball caps and sun visors. They mill at the bar and holler for more beer. On the wood-paneled walls hang dusty creels and fly rods. A petite blond waitress of about thirty races around like a gerbil. Her name is Stephanie.

"Barry, I told you," she snaps over her shoulder as she zooms past, "I'll bring you another one when I come back around."

Barry replies with something mildly suggestive.

When Stephanie finally makes it to our table, the first thing she says is "I'm out of the specials."

Ken and Russ and I acknowledge this in unison, though we are completely unaware of what the specials might have been or that they even existed.

"And just so you know," she adds curtly, "the kitchen is no longer serving chicken sandwiches, nachos, tacos or mussels."

Why anyone would come to a place like this to eat tacos and mussels is not explained. We order some burgers.

As we wait for our food, I feel disconnected, as though I am in two places at once. It is not a wholly unpleasant condition, but at that moment, I cannot put a name to it. Russ does it for me.

"I feel like we're still on the water," he observes, running an uneasy hand over his face.

That's what it is. When I close my eyes, I'm still rocking and bobbing in the boat.

"Well, we were floating for almost twelve hours," says Ken.

Ansel Adams, "The Tetons and the Snake River" (1942). *Grand Teton National Park, Wyoming. National Archives and Records Administration, Records of the National Park Service. (79-AAG-1).*

We nod and rub our eyes. Even in a high-tech fiberglass drift boat we are terrestrials adrift on a serpentine line of liquid time. Its currents push and pull us down the river, and they keep doing so long after we walk up onto land, get in the truck and go on home. In my mind, I am still there. In our minds, we are all still on every river we have ever fished. Once you fish a river, you can never really leave it.

There are shorter river sections we might have floated, but we chose the Canyon Section because it's twenty-five miles of river and because it would take a long time. That's what we came in search of—time. We found a single moment between past and future that would last us all day, and we let the river do the rest.

ALL THE FISH ARE UNDER WATER

ALL THE FISH ARE UNDER WATER

Chadd VanZanten

When I was in college, I worked as a sporting goods clerk at a department store. I'll be the first to admit it was not the best place in town to get fishing gear or hunting rifles. The store was better known for apparel and housewares, and our rather dingy little sporting goods department was more of a holding area for guys who'd wandered away while their wives tried on clothes.

We didn't have the amusement park amenities of today's big-box outdoor retailers, no attractions to keep our clientele occupied until someone came to collect them. We had no full-body taxidermy elk mounts or giant aquariums filled with twenty-inch trout. At one point, we did have a smelly old stuffed jackalope squatting small and sinister by the cash register. It didn't help. And we hung up a fake rubber fish that sang rock-n-roll songs at you when you poked it, but that got old in a hurry, too.

So, we set up a little TV and played fishing videos all day. It was, literally, the least we could do.

The most popular videos at the time were about bass fishing—programs with tragic production values but hosts who were folksy and enthusiastic. There was laid-back Jerry McKinnis, who hosted *The Fishin' Hole*, which first aired in 1963 and ran continually for an astonishing forty-four years. Then there was the self-effacing Tennessee boy Bill Dance, who would reel in a nine-pound bass in one scene and then fall out of his boat in the next.

One show featured a scale model of a lake made of fiberglass and papier-mâché. It was perhaps nine feet across, with little fake trees and rocks all around. The lake's surface was represented by a thin sheet of blue plastic on hinges. To enable the viewer to see what lay beneath the water, the host lifted the plastic sheet like the hood of a truck.

I'll never forget one line of the narration from that program, which the host delivered with a southern twang and completely without irony. As he opened his plastic lake to reveal the submerged tree stumps and sandbars, he said, "The hardest part about fishing is that all the fish are under water."

What I found most amusing about this bulletin is that it makes clear that *all* the fish are under water. Not just some. Not most. All.

And yet the observation is not without value. If anything, it's an understatement. It's not just the hardest part of fishing; it's one of the primary reasons we fish in the first place.

Humans have been transfixed by the watery world since the Stone Age discovery that oceans and rivers harbor rich stocks of strange and slippery creatures that might, with a little effort, be coaxed from their homes and then eaten.

In the past hundred years or so, we have turned slightly more philosophical about our aquatic counterparts, even though we still know very little about what goes on beneath the waves. Only a few hundred yards down there are things going on that no human eyes have witnessed.

The trout and salmon are winning us over, gradually. They say it's impossible to restore the trout and steelhead and salmon populations that existed before widespread human settlement and development, but we're at least building fewer dams, tearing some of them down and helping fish get around the ones we need.

A couple hundred years ago, my home waters teemed with Bonneville cutthroat trout, a fluvial species that grew to massive size in the mighty Bear River and choked the tributaries with its spawning runs. Then white settlers arrived in the 1850s. Their overfishing, deforestation and water developments pushed the cutthroat to within sight of extirpation. A tiny remnant of the species survived, though no one knows how. Throughout the 1900s, well-meaning conservation agencies tried to revive the depleted Bear River fishery by planting exotic species considered more productive and sporty—brown trout, panfish, carp—and the native cutts somehow weathered that, too, though by then, they were a remnant of a remnant. As

One reason we gather at the water's edge is because we can't exist beneath it. We can never truly enter it.

water and fish grow scarcer and scarcer across the West 150 years later, we begin to cherish what was here to begin with.

Whatever our stated motives, one reason we gather at the water's edge is because we can't exist beneath it. The thesis of the aforementioned fishing video might be better phrased like this: "The hardest thing about fishing is that all the people live on land." All of us. We approach the shore to peer into the murk and perhaps dive in, but eventually, we float to the top again. Even the most advanced underwater explorers merely cheat nature for short periods by creating small pockets of our world to take with them. There is no hinged hatchway to lift. We can never truly enter in.

We anglers connect with the aquatic world by hooking fish and bringing them to us, which places great demands on them. We deceive the fish, hassle them, force them into fighting for their lives. And we sometimes kill and eat them. I do what I can to compensate for my incursions—conservation efforts, mostly, with organizations like Trout Unlimited. If I pull some old tires from a riverbed or help restore native fish to historic habitat, I feel like I'm clear to fish every so often. It's a selfish and excessively human-oriented ideology, I know, but if I retreat too much further, I just might talk myself out of fishing altogether.

When I was a young boy, of course, my opinion was more focused. I thought the fish existed to be captured. Outwitting the quickest and most elusive of creatures on their own turf impressed me as a great achievement,

The Cub is well secluded, and although it can be brushy and challenging to fish, the odds of landing a one-pound cutthroat in full, post-spawn livery are reasonable.

the reward for which was possessing the fish, holding it in my hand to feel its weight and movement.

One day some time ago, I excused myself from work for that purpose: to hold a fish in my hand. I packed some provisions and headed for southeastern Idaho and the Cub River, which emerges from the side of a mountain as if a thirsty Moses had struck the rock there.

The Cub is small water. It drains only about thirty square miles of arid Idaho mountain range and seldom runs higher than seven hundred cubic feet per second at peak flow. Fittingly, it's a tributary to the Bear River. But the Cub is well secluded, and although it can be brushy and challenging to fish, the odds of landing a one-pound cutthroat in full post-spawn livery are reasonable.

The water was somewhat colored that day, and I saw no risers. It was not a day for sight-fishing. Instead, I prospected likely holding water to induce strikes by fish guessed at but unseen. I floated my fly over one such spot without success, and then I fished out the cast, not because I thought there might be a fish farther downstream, but out of habit. However, as the fly glided over the shallower, less-promising water, the gravelly streambed quavered, resolved into a cutthroat trout and rose up. This fish was not just an inhabitant of the stream but an actual unpieced sliver of it.

I did not know this when I was young, but I have since learned the true satisfaction of fishing is less about cleverness and control and more about bridging air and water. That's why I want to see the fish take a dry fly from the surface and why I holler when a big fish leaps into the air.

As long as a fish is on my line, we are connected between two worlds.

When I placed the cutthroat back into the tea-colored water, he sidled sleepily away from the bank. After a few seconds, he seemed to awaken and then darted back to his mid-current lie with the urgency only a fleeing trout can exhibit. When the cutthroat stopped, his edges vanished, and he was lost from my view. The trout that had lain cool and slick in my hand only a few seconds before had joined the stream again.

Nowadays, it is not as important for me to hold the fish as it is to watch it return to its water. No matter how many times it happens, communing with a creature that has crossed from one world to another and back again is reassuring in ways that are difficult to explain. Answers lie in such communion. It may, in fact, say something about the nature and future of our souls.

WHERE THEY AREN'T

Chadd VanZanten

A large part of finding out where the fish are is finding out where they aren't.
—*John Gierach*

During World War II, if you found yourself a member of a long-range bomber crew flying missions over Germany, it was time to get your affairs in order. Get right with your maker. There was a fifty-fifty chance you wouldn't be coming home.

It's not that each individual mission was so very dangerous; your chance of surviving one bombing run was something like 95 percent. Sometimes, it seems like driving across Wyoming with Utah plates on my truck is more hazardous than that. But each crew had to fly twenty-five missions before they could go home, so compound a 5 percent probability of dying by twenty-five independent events. That's 50 percent. We call that "even money."

In an attempt to sweeten the odds for its airmen, the British Air Ministry decided to fit its aircraft with armor. The question was where to put it? There are so many places on an airplane that are vulnerable to damage—the engines, the control surfaces, the pilot's internal organs. But you can't encase a whole plane in armor. If you did, you'd have what's known in the military-industrial complex as a "tank."

So, the Air Ministry collected data on bombers that had gotten shot up while flying over Germany. Pretty soon, they had a very good statistical picture of where their airplanes were most likely to get shot. They supposed the next step was pretty simple: put armor over those spots, and the planes would be protected.

But that was a bad idea. And someone said so.

The guy's name was Abraham Wald, a mathematician from Hungary. Here's what he noticed: the Air Ministry did not examine planes that had been shot down. How could they? Those planes were at the bottom of the English Channel. Instead, the data was collected only from planes that had been hit but kept on flying. Wald pointed out that if they put armor on the places where surviving planes had been shot, they'd succeed only in protecting the planes from hits they'd probably survive anyway, leaving their vulnerable areas still unprotected. I'll give you a couple seconds to read that again.

Instead, Wald said, put armor on the places where surviving planes were free of damage. Find the bullet holes, and put the armor where they aren't. Logically, those are the places where the shot-down planes had been fatally hit.

Long story short, the plan worked. The Air Ministry armored up its planes as Wald suggested, and things actually got a little better for the airmen. And the case itself is still something of a monument to overcoming fallacy and bias when considering statistical data.

There are two reasons I carry this lesson around with me. First, I think it remarks quite elegantly on the nature of the universe. Second, it helped me catch a fish one time.

Wald knew that sometimes the situation is very, very complicated. There are times when it's stupid to keep it simple. Looking at some airplanes, noticing the bullet holes and putting armor over them seems right until you realize the complexity of the situation.

Fortunately, just because something is complicated doesn't mean it's impossible to understand. If you're like me, as soon as you heard Wald's reasoning, it made perfect sense. As soon as I realized that it involved a sort of backward-thinking process, it clicked.

When I was first learning to fly-fish, very few things clicked. My mind reeled with the complexity of the supposedly elegant pursuit I'd taken up. Lines, casting, flies, fish—numerous volumes have been written about each one, and those are just a few basic headings. Yet the fly angler must develop a working familiarity with all those subjects and a considerable number of others to begin connecting with fish with any degree of reliability.

In those early days, I may have allowed the daunting learning curve of fly-fishing psyche me out. I often thought I would never really understand any of it. I fished a lot of days without laying eyes on a single fish, and there were days when I saw fish in every direction but never hooked one.

At some point, I started thinking backward about it. It was in wintertime, and I had been told at the fly shop that fishing a size-22 Griffith's Gnat on still water in January could be productive on my home water. This sounded absurd. I thought there was a high likelihood that the guys at the shop had some sort of bet to see how crazy a story they could sell to the next customer who walked through the door. However, I was also very short on ideas about how to catch a fish. Never underestimate the gullibility of an angler who is deep in a dry spell. So, I gave up trying to detect if the shop guys were on the verge of cracking up. I gave up all skepticism, in fact. At that point, I'd have taken advice from a four-year-old kid. I listened carefully, bought the flies they told me to and then went to the place they pointed to on a map.

There I stood, casting this utterly invisible fly for a couple hours in the core-freezing cold over a flat-calm backwater. After two or three hours, I was ready to go home, skunked again. Then, all at once, a brown trout took the fly almost without showing its nose above the water. I set the hook, and somehow, it stayed in the fish. I had yet to learn that those small flies come away as often as they stick. This time it stuck. The fish dove into some deep water, and I held onto the rod. That was my entire strategy—hold onto the rod.

At the time, I hadn't caught more than twenty fish on the fly, so my ability to judge the size of the fish was poor. They all seemed pretty big to me. He would have surely broken off if he'd played even one dirty trick, like turning into the current, ducking under the ice or making one decent jump.

But he didn't. He just ran up and down the backwater about eleven times, turned on his side and allowed me to scoop him up.

The trout was as big and heavy as any three fish I'd ever caught on fly gear. He convulsed a couple times in the small net and nearly wrenched the handle out of my hand. I didn't realize what a prize he was until a couple years later when I told a much more seasoned angler the story.

"How big was it?" he asked.

I held my hands about twenty inches apart. Then I moved them out a couple inches. Then back in a few.

But I didn't care because that was the day I started thinking backward about it.

"At Spring Hollow," he said, eyes narrow.

"Uh huh," I said. "Just up from that big gravel bar. In the backwater."

He didn't refute the story. He was too polite to do that. But judging from his expression, he thought I was a big fat liar.

I didn't care. There was some luck involved, sure, and it was a long time before I caught a fish like that in the same place again. But I didn't care because that was the day I started thinking backward about it. I started thinking about where they're not, and where they shouldn't be but often are. That's the day I realized that fishing for three days with no fish had somehow prepared me to accept the preposterous, and that's why I hooked that big brown. At last, I had it in my head that the complex aspects of fly-fishing could be understood and that a day with no fish can teach one just as much as days when you land a lunker.

Spring Hollow Bridge on the Logan River.

A Curtis Creek Bonneville cutthroat trout.

Willow Flats on the Cub River between seasons.

The Henry's Fork of the Snake River.

Jason Reed. Oh, and a cutthroat.

Opposite, top: A Cinnamon Creek brown trout.

Opposite, bottom: A rare rest for Bradley between netting fish.

Above: The
Mighty Mo.

Left: The Council
of the Tyers.

The Cub River.

Blacksmith Fork River.

Opposite and top: Wind Rivers Range.

Bradley in his new drift boat.

Missouri River Rainbow.

Black Canyon section of the Bear River.

Logan Canyon, Utah. *Photo by Paul Hermans.*

Wasatch Mountains. Bowman Fork. *Photo by Scott Brill.*

Wasatch Mountains. Bowman Fork. *Photo by Scott Brill.*

The Clark Fork River. *Bureau of Land Management.*

Wellsville Mountains, arial view, Cache Valley, Utah. *Photo by Steve Sellers.*

Wind River Range. *Photo by Andy Porter.*

Snake River. *Photo by Daniel Mayer.*

Fremont Peak in the Wind River Range. *Photo by Ben Grasseschi.*

Bitterroot River. *Photo by Doug Kueffler.*

Tenkar fishing on the Cub River.

AND HE SAITH UNTO THEM, FOLLOW ME, AND I WILL MAKE YOU FISHERS OF MEN (MATTHEW 4:19)

BELIEF, LUCK AND LIES

Russ Beck

He placed the fly on my palm like a priest administering the Eucharist.

"What's it called again?"

He told me and gave me the basic recipe.

"One more thing," he said, "don't tell anyone about this fly."

"Right." I put my finger to my nose, winked and laughed.

He forced a laugh but interrupted it with, "No, seriously though." He looked me in the eyes. "Don't tell anyone about this fly."

I stopped laughing.

"It consistently outfishes all my other flies on any river in the valley."

I nodded.

"I'm going to need to hear you promise."

"I promise."

Other anglers have similar stories or flies. Everyone has a secret spot that they will not share, even with close friends. And it makes sense. Angling is steeped in belief, luck and lies. Flies themselves are lies, and the fish are, too, sometimes. Anything that is so predicated on uncertainty and lies must have its secrets, its rituals, its demanded sacrifices.

I placed my friend's fly in my box and immediately forgot about it until a day on the Blacksmith Fork River. There was a small mayfly hatch occurring

In accordance with a vow Russ has taken, the fly depicted is not the one mentioned in the essay.

(small in terms of size of the mayflies and their numbers), and I fished to the risers. I couldn't catch them. I switched from a size-18 Renegade to a size-16 Parachute Adams. Nothing. As an afterthought, I tied on my friend's secret fly as a dropper. As soon as the flies touched the water, I saw the Adams dip, and the secret fly produced a ten-inch brown. I didn't think much of it because I knew I should be catching fish at the spot. I wiggled him off the hook and cast to the same spot. This time, I pulled in a fourteen-inch rainbow on the secret fly. I unhooked him, popped off the dry and fished the secret fly with an indicator. Year-round, the fly simply always produces. I have yet to be skunked with it. It's the closest thing I have to a talisman on the river.

But it's not the fly. It's the secret and the confidence in that secret. I understand why we keep secrets about spots on the river—too much traffic can physically alter a fishing hole or chase the fish away. I'm less clear about why we hush up about flies.

Some say if fish see the same lures, they'll eventually learn, but I can't buy that a single fish could get enough exposure to a single fly to know that it's no longer food. I think it has much more to do with faith than the fish themselves. We are wired to believe that what is secret is sacred. It's the sacred nature of the secret that makes us fish with confidence, and that confidence is more productive than any learned technique.

Brad wills fish onto the line.

"You will catch a fish in that pool," he says. "They are there. Oh, perfect cast. That will produce. See? See?"

He's always right. His belief conjures fish.

My wife's boss sent me an article by Samuel Snyder titled "New Streams of Religion: Fly Fishing as a Lived, Religion of Nature." I edged my way through the essay reluctantly. I usually try to avoid topics like this because it turns fishing into something that I just can't get behind. Such texts sometimes cover up what fishing is at its core: smartish beings tricking dumber ones. There's a lot that goes into that trick: waders that can cost $1,000, planned trips away from family and learning to craft flies out of feather and lead. They're all just tricks.

However, as Snyder waxed about the rituals and the texts and the baptisms and the meditations, I may have let out a small, involuntary "hallelujah." If you loosen up definitions and take some sweeping liberties, you can see how fly-fishing can be its own set of beliefs and rituals based on results and testimony, the purpose of which is to order the chaos—a religion. Perhaps where it connects most firmly with religion is through belief. Every fly, fishing trip and false cast is based on a belief that it will somehow produce a fish.

If you isolate each step, fly-fishing seems ridiculous. You have to throw in a pinch of something unexplained for it to make sense.

With a little prodding, fly-fishing can move past just faith and fish production and into actual miracles. One of my favorite authors, Scott Carrier, talks about angling in his essay "The Test." This is the only piece in which I've heard him mention fishing—and maybe it's because, as he says, "talking about fishing is silly, like farting and tap dancing at the same time." Toward the end Carrier says, "It was the fly rod—just holding the rod in [my] hand, that cured [me]."

Here is something I know is true: my dad's family are known as witchers. In his compact truck, behind the seat, he keeps two copper rods about half a centimeter in diameter bent into uppercase *L*s. He can walk around your property with the rods held parallel, lightly bouncing in his hands. When the rods clank together, he'll look up and tell you that if you want to find water, it's best to dig there, directly beneath where the rods came together.

I once asked him how it works.

He said, "I don't really know, it just does."

Apparently, his dad could not only find water but also tell people how far to dig to get to it. The idea of rivers flowing underground that are somehow summoned is something I really want to believe in.

I dated a girl who's dad dug wells for a living. She said that he used both hydrologists and witchers to find water—one, she said, was about as accurate (and as expensive) as the other. When Dad picks a well spot, he tells the landowners that it probably won't work, that they should definitely get a second opinion. But he's never wrong. He does this only for people he knows and won't charge a fee because, I think, he's still surprised it actually works and perhaps because it contradicts his line of work—he holds a PhD in chemistry. He consults for exorbitant fees about carpet cleaners, antibacterial scrubs and even alchemy. If he were to somehow buy into the mystical aspects of his witching, would he have to trade in his credentials and bloated paychecks? I've asked Dad to teach me how to witch, but we've never gotten around to it. Personally, I don't think I have it in me. And I'm not sure what he'd actually teach. He doesn't slip into a trance or chant anything. Minus the rods, when he witches, it looks just like his going for a fairly normal, if a little jagged, stroll. He used to teach, and his skeptical students and peers asked for a demonstration. He walked around his college's quad with a maintenance man and mapped all the buried sprinkler lines. Many still didn't believe him, but how could they?

Fishing is all about mixing the mystical with the scientific. Some anglers dig deep into the science. They take entomology classes and count abdominal segments on aquatic insect larva. They have detailed calendars filled with weather reports, flow levels and calculations.

I fished a small, clear creek on private land with a tenkara rod and an elk-hair caddis.

Others steep in the mystical and have lucky hats and puffy, purple flies. They're more concerned with the numbers on the calendar than moon phases. When it comes to faith and fishing, I think I have to claim to be an agnostic angler. Sometimes, I may be willing to believe there's something mystical, something unexplained that attracts fish to hooks, but if I'm hard pressed, I'll side with science.

But not always. Sometimes there's something else that even the skeptic in me can't explain away. Tonight, my back is sore from casting. I fished a small, clear creek on private land with a tenkara rod and an elk-hair caddis. The creek was seldom wider than I am tall, and the water pushed past round rocks. I caught an old, cranky brown trout. His head was shaped like a doorstop. His back was boney, and his adipose fin hung limp like wrinkles off an old woman's arm. I'm sure he had never been caught before. I'm not sure how I know this fact, but I do.

Rule 6

SIMON PETER SAITH UNTO THEM, I GO A FISHING, THEY SAY UNTO HIM, WE ALSO GO WITH THEE, THEY WENT FORTH AND ENTERED INTO A SHIP IMMEDIATELY AND THAT NIGHT THEY CAUGHT NOTHING (JOHN 21:3)

THE IRON ROD

Russ Beck

"If they ask, just say you're here to cook dinner. We need people to cook dinner—and I'll even throw you a potato to peel."

"Are they going to ask?"

"No. Probably not. Maybe." Chadd paused longer than made me comfortable. "No, they won't."

"Are we doing something bad?"

"I don't think so."

When Chadd told me about fishing at the Cinnamon Creek campground, it was always with a reverent and wistful tone. He told stories of big, eager browns, rainbows and cutthroats that practically ran into your net. The land was owned by the Mormon Church and hardly ever got fished. Chadd worked at the camp in the summer, which gave him a pass into the campground and earned him the privilege of fishing there. He helped pitch tents and cook food for dozens of young Mormon boys in training to go on into missionary service all over the world. And if the big fish weren't enough, it was the only place for a hundred miles where you could catch Kokanee salmon.

I wanted in. I wanted in so bad that I knew I would lie for it.

The lady at the gate asked who I was with. When I answered, I realized it wasn't a test; she just wanted to give good directions. She was soft

I wanted in. I wanted in so bad that I knew I would lie for it.

with age and quick to smile and laugh. She noticed the fishing gear in my backseat.

"You think you'll get a chance to fish?" she asked. "They keep the leaders pretty busy."

"I hope so. Do you know any place that's good?"

"Well, jeeze." She waved her hand toward the creek. "Take your pick. They're everywhere."

As I drove into the campground, I noticed the young men weren't wearing the grubby jeans and T-shirts I expected. Instead, they all wore white shirts and ties. And the campgrounds weren't bushy with dirt trails. It was manicured green lawns and bark-covered walkways. I drove slowly so that I wouldn't kick up dust and soil their Sunday best.

Chadd waved me over from the edge of the camp, where he pulled on his waders.

He watched me watch the kids, "Oh, hell, it's not that weird."

We put in just above a footbridge. The creek was gin clear with rust-colored rocks the size and shape of bowling balls. Willows and cottonwoods choked the banks. The bottom wiggled with fish that were mostly concealed by the color of the rocks.

A man in a vintage three-piece suit stood on the bridge. His wiry gray hair probably hadn't been combed since he got to camp a few days before. He watched us through aged yellow eyeglasses as we tied on our flies.

"Do you think you'll catch any?"

Chadd shrugged. "Probably. Well, I hope so."

"You're a little confident." He chuckled and winked at us. "Nothing's guaranteed, boys."

I could tell he didn't trust our rods. Most people don't believe in fly angling—including most fly anglers. We try to get past the thought that our skill is just a rough-hewn mix of luck and charlatanism. But chief among the disbelievers is the casual spin angler, and I'd bet this guy was one of those. He'd probably fished thirty times in his life and maybe caught fish ten of those times. The rods and gear look more complicated and less effective to the casual angler.

Chadd had a fish on before the guy crossed the bridge. I looked back at the man and tried to not look smug. I'm pretty sure it didn't work.

Alongside the stream was a hard-packed dirt trail with a metal handrail. Brush had been cleared almost too aggressively from the trail. For some reason the incongruity of a handrail next to this small trail out in the middle of nowhere didn't register with me. But as Chadd and I stood in the stream lining up our next shot, another leader in a white shirt and tie came up the trail and explained that he would be leading a group of boys along the trail shortly.

"I'd appreciate it if you could keep it down," he said.

I nodded and pretended to know what he was talking about.

Chadd asked the leader if we should get out of the creek and go upstream so that we wouldn't interfere. The leader insisted we'd be fine, but he asked us, again, to keep it quiet.

Minutes later, a line of blindfolded teens in white shirts arrived, stumbling along the path and holding on to the handrail. They weren't talking or laughing. If anything, they looked scared. They bit their lips and held tight to the rod.

I looked to Chadd for an explanation, and he just shrugged. As per our orders, he couldn't do much more than that.

In it, the ancient prophet Lehi sees the Tree of Life in a vision.

The groping teens were re-creating a scene from the Book of Mormon. In it, the ancient prophet Lehi sees the Tree of Life in a vision. The tree produces a delicious heavenly fruit, which represents salvation. But for Lehi and his family to reach it, they must pass through a thick mist. To get through the mist and to the tree, God provides an iron rod, like a handrail. In Mormonism, holding on to the rod symbolizes staying true to the word of God. Also in the vision, a river runs parallel to the path, and on the other side a large building looms with people laughing and pointing at those holding the rod. Only the unfaithful let go of the rod and tried to ford the river to be with the people in the building, but they drowned.

We both got in to fish at the same time—they stumbled over each other for the fly, taking it as soon as it alighted on the water. It was the kind of fishing that one wants to scream about, but we stayed dumb. We attempted to pull in fish after fish silently, so as to not disturb the blindfolded teens tripping and grasping the rail just feet away. All we could do was look at each other and smile, our eyebrows buried in the shade of our baseball caps.

The effect of this activity on the kids, I imagine, was pretty powerful. They hear water flowing near them but can't see it. The only thing keeping their feet dry is the rod.

Chadd and I completed the metaphor, playing the role of the unfaithful who veered from the path and taunted as the righteous pressed on. The leaders should have told us not to be quiet but, instead, to succumb to our natural inclination, which was to laugh at the teens and holler when we pulled in trout. We were mostly quiet, but I suspect they heard fish flapping in nets and our whispered conversations.

The truth is I *am* the one who veered, in the church camp metaphor and in life. I lied to be calf-deep in that perfect stream, and less abstractly, I left the Mormon Church in my twenties. If anyone should have been in that stream to warn the teens, it was me.

I dipped into the water gradually. It started when I was a teenager in all-night conversations about religion with my best friend. He would later become a vocal atheist and critic of the Mormon Church. But when he left the church, I stayed. I still loved it. It's the faith that inspired my ancestors to leave comfortable lives in Europe and walk across a continent (yes, including Nebraska). That's why it took me until my midtwenties to stop going to church, long after I'd stopped believing. Entering grad school seemed like the right time to exit my faith. That's when and where I met my wife, too.

After we married, we lived in a defunct Mormon church in rural Idaho. The incongruity of non-believers living in a house of God was not lost on us. It felt wrong cleaning up my dog's shit from the perfect wood floors in the apartment. Our landlord gave us keys to the chapel to store our bicycles, and we found a half dozen disused toilets next to pews. Dead mice were scattered on the floor like toys in a nursery.

My wife, who was also raised in the Mormon Church, felt some fidelity to the faith that I had lost, so we made a pact: every Sunday we would go either to church or to the mountains. I deferred to her because if it were up to me, it would be mountains every week—starched button-down white shirts have always fit my body strangely.

She usually picked mountains, but we kept the same mantra ("church or mountains") for a couple years. Eventually, the mantra mutated to "mountains or movies," and that's where it stayed.

I've always hated the expression "lost my faith," like it was a set of keys or an old book. I know exactly where my faith is, and I could go and find it any time. It's in that chapel that I avoid on Sundays and with my parents and sisters. The truth is, I'm more comfortable with those in the water, any water, than those sitting in the pews.

Despite my mom's fears, there may still be hope for me. There's a slight problem with a mixed metaphor in the primary text of the iron-rod allegory. The water in the vision both drowns those who veer but is also seen as "the fountain of living waters…which waters are a representation of the love of God." I like that the river is murky. That it's both good and bad. But even if the water was gin-clear bad, given the options of going to church and staying dry or wading into a river that one day will probably kill me, I'd walk toward the river every time.

After Moses parted the waters and killed thousands of Egyptians, he didn't have a temple to commune with God, so he hiked up a mountain and watched God's finger write the ten commandments on stone. I could lie and say that I'm in the mountains hiking the streams to find God and the faith I misplaced, but I'm not. Most of my spirituality evaporated out of me, but if God were to talk to me, it wouldn't be in a church (because I wouldn't be there), it would be on a remote mountain creek miles from the nearest chapel.

When the boys finally got out of earshot, Chadd and I talked about the fishing—but nothing much needed to be said. It felt downright holy, and it had little to do with the proximity to the path, the rod or the camp. We fished higher, and the stream got smaller but never too small to hold fish.

Chadd asked me if I had ever been to a camp like this when I was growing up.

"Me? No."

That night I didn't stay to peel potatoes. I snuck off the mountain with a sore back and a phone filled with photographs of trout. But Chadd stayed. I can hear the dad jokes he told to the teens and can taste the Dutch-oven stew he made (maybe too heavy with garlic). He found a way to be both in the river and near the path. But the next morning, after breakfast, before everyone broke camp, I imagine Chadd put together his rod and slipped deep into that creek.

YOUR PLAN? IT SUCKS

FINAL PLAN F

Chadd VanZanten

The original plan was for the four of us to backpack into the Wind River Range and fish for four days—me, my son Klaus, my buddy Brad and Brad's buddy Chris.

Four of us for four days. That was the plan.

The four-man fishing trip has a certain elegance. Four people can furnish good company without stepping on each other's feet. A four-man team also fits perfectly into one SUV, so you can split gas money, and if you encounter a bear, odds are decent it will eat one of your friends instead of you. The four-man team is simple, efficient.

But plans fall apart. It's what they do.

This one crumbled when another of Brad's buddies asked to join us, and Brad obliged. I don't even remember the guy's name. But because we could no longer fit in one vehicle, we split into two teams, with each group driving separately.

This was Plan B.

Nobody panicked. Two teams in separate vehicles actually adds flexibility to a trip like this. For example, it enables part of the group to leave early or stay longer. Having two vehicles instead of one is also more convenient in the event that one of the two drivers is devoured by a bear. You might say that our backup plan was marginally better than the original.

The original plan was for the four of us to backpack into the Wind River Range and fish for four days.

But backup plans fall apart, too.

Chris needed to move the trip up one day because of his work schedule, but I couldn't go any earlier because of mine, so we created Plan C—the two teams would drive up on consecutive days and fish together during the two-day overlap. It was not ideal but not tragic as far as backup-backup plans go, but soon we moved on to Plan D when Klaus had to cancel altogether because he'd forgotten he had swim team practice. Plan D survived only briefly before Plan E was hatched so that Brad could leave an additional day early for reasons I've forgotten.

According to Plan E, I would leave home on Sunday, hike in on Monday and meet up with Brad's team that afternoon. Unfortunately, I was delayed by one extra day because of a minor case of engine trouble. But it's meaningless to keep track of the backup plans from here on because by then, Brad was in the mountains and we couldn't communicate with anything less than satellite phones, and we had no satellite phones.

Under the terms of what I will designate "Final Plan F," I hiked in a day and a half late with the intention of somehow finding Brad, but Brad's team was meanwhile plagued by a variety of hardships, including heavy rain and a case of violent diarrhea, which caused them to hike out after only three days, which meant we missed each other completely.

I wasn't heartbroken that the original plan of teamwork and company lay in utter shambles. I love fishing alone. With an entire week off, I could stay as long as my food held out, and I figured I could force it to hold out for a long time.

I actually got fairly excited about it. That didn't last.

It was still raining a little that first day, but as soon as it cleared up, I grabbed my fly rod and fished a nearby lake, where the exuberance of the resident brook trout was surpassed only by their sheer numbers. With no traveling companions to answer to, I realized I could fish for the rest of the day if I wanted to. So I did.

Back at my campsite, I pulled on a jacket against the evening chill, and then I unpacked my foodstuffs. The lack of dinnertime banter was a bit discouraging, but I told myself this could also pass for tranquility.

For dinner, I had a custom-made dehydrated casserole of potatoes, bacon and veggies. I'd used the recipe before, and although the pre-packed ingredients required only the addition of boiling water, I figured I must have committed some grave error in its preparation because the first mouthful was only slightly more appetizing than moistened pocket lint.

As I choked it down, I made an important discovery about subsisting in the wilderness: having company really helps you lie to yourself about how the food tastes. When you're with a buddy, even if the food is crummy, you say, "You know, this doesn't taste too bad." And he agrees—"Yeah, the crumbled bacon was a great idea." Without companionship, every meal tastes exactly as good as it really is, which of course is usually somewhere in the vicinity of "not very."

Having company really helps you lie to yourself about how the food tastes.

No campfires were allowed that year, and the short-lived flames of my cookstove made a poor substitute. Without fire or friend, I sat watching the night draw a black hood over my campsite, and I formed misgivings about my ability to pass a week in so lonesome a condition.

I'd seen solo backpackers before. I saw several on the hike in. Soloing never struck me as particularly demanding—I assumed I could do it if I wanted to, but between my sons and friends, the opportunity had never presented itself. In my tent that night, I thought a lot about my two boys and how it would be to be fishing with them. I thought about how fun it is to fish with Brad. And I'd never even met Chris, but I thought quite a bit about him, too.

In the morning, the sun rose over the valley, and I started to look on the bright side again. As I warmed up a cup of cocoa, I laid plans for a full day of solitary fishing. I identified a stream to explore, and with my tenkara rod, I soon discovered that it held equal numbers of cutthroat and brook trout.

It was a noisy stream, with lots of riffles and rapids, so instead of the hair-and-feather flies I prefer, I tied on a gaudy, foam-bodied object with rubber legs and a shiny foil wing. Any actual insect would have regarded it as shamefully overdressed, but the cutts and brookies practically took turns at the fly, as though they might be under some kind of truce.

Most were small, twelve inches and down. However, as is usually the case in the Winds, I was able to hook a few larger fish, one of which was seventeen inches or thereabouts. But such good fortune is less satisfying when you're alone. A great fish is always greater when there's a witness to it.

With every fish I brought to hand, I checked the progress of the sun to ensure enough daylight remained for a few more casts. Hiking around in the dark in the Wind Rivers isn't exactly death defying, but it's not to be taken lightly either, especially when you're alone.

To our primitive ancestors, night wasn't the respite it is to us. Today's man sees the setting sun as a signal to sit down and turn on the television. To our ancestors, night was just another hazard to cope with, as threatening as any rival or predator. When you are alone at night in a very remote place, you may not be gripped with the same fear felt by ancient man, but you'll get a taste of it, and I got mine that evening. As I hiked back to camp, I saw the face and forepaws of some large mammal emerging suddenly from the brush a few yards ahead. I knew instantly that it was a bear, and I was resigned to becoming the subject of news reports and magazine articles recounting my struggle for survival against one of the only North American apex predators that is not afraid of man. I'm still not sure how I avoided wetting my pants, dropping everything and running like scared cat.

However, in the failing light I eventually identified the creature as a porcupine, a very distant cousin to any animal that could do me harm. Even so, I stood frozen on the trail as it shambled away murmuring.

And so a second day of solo fishing was followed by a second evening of gloomy stillness, and the third day and evening passed in much the same way. There was again no fire and no one to watch fire with, so I turned in shortly after dark. I'd hardly made a dent in my rations, but I realized I couldn't last the rest of the week no matter how many Clif Bars I had remaining. Before I'd gotten all the way into my sleeping bag, I'd decided to abandon Final Plan F in favor of just heading home. I lay there for a long time staring at the top vent of my tent where a little starlight leaked in.

My least favorite thing about backpacking is breaking down my tent and packing away my gear, so in the morning, I slept later than I intended.

Then voices woke me up. People voices.

I poked my head out of the tent and squinted. There were four of them, coming up single file from the main trail by the lake in the valley floor: a guy about my age leading two teenagers and an older guy bringing up the rear. They laughed and joked as they approached. Each carried a fishing rod, and although unannounced social calls are generally unheard of in the backcountry, I got it in my head that they were coming to visit me for some reason. So I hastily dressed myself.

They weren't coming to visit, of course. There was a footpath that wound past my campsite and went on to a small lake a mile or so up into the hills. But still I made it out of the tent and was sitting on the ground tying up my boots when they passed by.

"Hello," called the guy in the lead. "Nice morning, huh?"

I'd been trying so hard to act like I'd only just noticed them, I inadvertently answered, "Good!"

In my defense, I'll point out that I hadn't spoken much in the previous seventy-two hours. I'd said, "Hi" to a couple hikers on the trail the first day, and I think I said, "Good as it gets" the next day when a college kid asked me how the fishing had been.

"I mean, good morning," I stammered.

The lead guy chuckled and nodded.

"Going up to Blue Lake?" I asked before they got out of earshot.

They didn't want to stop and talk, I could see that, but the lead guy slowed down a little.

"Yep," he said over his shoulder. "Ever been up there?"

"Sure, yeah," I said. "The fishing's great."

That stopped them.

"How great?"

"Yeah, and how far is it?" asked the older guy.

I looked up the hill and pursed my lips. "Mile," I said. "But this trail doesn't really go all the way up. It's hard to follow once you get to the boulders, and it's kind of a climb. But the fishing?" I held up my hands. "Ridiculous."

They traded glances, nodding and grinning.

"What do you use up there?"

"What do you got?" I asked.

They hurried over and surrendered their tackle for inspection. Apparently, they were visiting after all.

The younger guy and his son were fly anglers. The older guy and the other boy had spin gear.

"These spinners will work," I said, pointing. "Jigs'll work. Got any streamers? Good. Definitely use those. And just about any of these big dries will catch something. They climb all over these."

"What's up there? Browns?"

"Brookies."

"Is it hard to find?" The older guy was sweating a little already.

"Not really, but you might want to go up the ravine instead. It's a longer hike but you can follow the creek right to the lake."

"How much longer?"

"Mile and a half, maybe. It's tricky. It's boulders all the way up."

"Hm."

"Just go slow," I said. "You'll be fine. If I can make it, you can."

They pocketed up their boxes and thanked me.

"I'm Dennis," said the lead guy. He introduced the others. Tanner, Jay and the older fellow was Boyd. We shook hands.

"So," said Dennis, "you heading up there today? Want to come with us?"

"Thanks," I said, "but no. I'm heading home after breakfast."

"You by yourself?" he asked, looking around for other tents.

"Yep," I said. I may have put my hands on my hips and stood a little taller. They nodded, raised their eyebrows.

"You don't get nervous up here alone?" asked Boyd.

"Nope," I answered—a little too quickly.

"Well, we'll be up there all day if you change your mind."

They thanked me again, and I watched them file off up the ravine.

A great fish is always greater when there's a witness to it.

I set up my stove and laid out some breakfast fixings, pausing now and again to scan the hillside and mark the probable progress of Dennis and his party. They seemed like a nice bunch of fellows. I replayed our conversation in my head, hoping I hadn't understated the difficulty of the climb or overstated the excellence of the fishing.

Sunlight burned away the dew, and a mist rose in the glare. All around me, the valley lay quiet and smoking like some prehistoric landscape, with only my tent and meager gear to suggest otherwise. Down in the floor of the valley, the fish in the lake began their morning rise.

When I'd finished my cocoa and rinsed the cooking gear, I stood over my tent and considered pulling up the first aluminum stake. I may have even bent down to get started. But I didn't. Instead, I packed a lunch, put on a hat and grabbed my fly rod.

Plans fall through all the time. It's what they do.

They're Always for Me

Russ Beck

Pam said she wanted something to make Nate feel involved in their wedding, something just for him. Nate's an Idaho game warden and a fly angler, so I said I'd make flies for their table favors.

I started out tying flies that I would actually use. I favor small flies: size-18 Parachute Adams, size-22 Pheasant Tails. I envisioned these gnat-sized flies embedded in the fingertips of drunk elderly family members and began to mash down the barbs with a little more vigor.

Eventually, I changed things up. Every time I tied, I would tie a handful for myself and then increase the size of whatever I was tying and throw some in the wedding pile. This worked, but some of them were still a little too subtle, too small. They eventually migrated into my fly box.

"Tie something frilly," my wife suggested.

"I don't fish with frilly flies."

"They're not for you."

"But there're going to be gamey people there, people who know how to fly fish: game wardens, sportsmen."

"There will be like three of those."

Pam confirmed this—so, I changed again. I bought a fifty-pack of size-6 Mustad hooks with heavy shanks and eyes I could fit my fly line through. I've caught fish smaller than those Mustads. Because I don't tie flies that big, I still had thread and wire that were mostly for the smaller flies. The flies I made with the giant hooks and subtle dressings are probably among my favorite that I've ever tied. I'm pretty sure none of them will get wet.

I did more shopping with the wedding flies in mind. At the fly shop, as I thumbed through brass beads, I had the thought, "These white beads would really make my chartreuse Woolly Buggers pop." I had to change the way I thought about flies, so I stopped thinking about what appeals to fish and started thinking about what appeals to a bride and groom. And the bride? She digs chartreuse.

As I checked out with my purple marabou and hunter-orange antron, the guy at the till chuckled. "Damn. What the hell are you tying?"

"It's not for me, man."

In addition to tying my own flies, I furl my own leaders, and I've built a rod (with a lot of help from a friend). When I first branched out into fishy hobbies, I thought I might move away from fishing—that hasn't happened

"Tie something frilly," my wife suggested.

yet. Plenty of people get caught up in the extra things and eventually wean themselves off fishing completely. There's a guy in my local Trout Unlimited chapter who knows everything about the bugs on the local rivers. He also cuts his own hair. When he goes to the river, he no longer takes his rod. Instead, he packs specimen bottles. Go to a fly-tying convention and talk to the tiers. Find out how many of them still fish. In *The Longest Silence*, Thomas McGuane writes about a casting club that's been meeting for decades at casting pools in Golden Gate Park. These casters never wet their lines on a river but can throw a tighter loop than any actual angler. To me, they represent a metaphor that lost its tenor.

When I fish with flies I've tied and leaders I've furled, I feel connected. When I turn thread around a hook, I think about fishing. When I twist those threads and watch them bind together, I see the river. This is why when I tied those flies for my friends' wedding, I suffered a sort of vertigo. I couldn't see the river—I had to see them. I wonder whom or what professional tiers see, the river or their customers?

I believe these extra activities make it so when I do fish, I fish better. I have a feeling angling anglers are regularly outfished by fishy-hobby anglers, even if fishy-hobby anglers spend less time on the river than angling anglers. (For the record, I'm not asking for a challenge from angling anglers. But my buddy Brad's fishy hobbies included a water-insect graduate class and a master's thesis on western rivers—I'll put him up against any angling angler any day.)

When I really got into fly tying, one of the first flies I tied was a size-16 Purple Haze. It had a moose-hair tail and grizzly hackles. I caught more trout on that single fly than on any other. Because it was one of my first flies, I embedded it with sentimentality and a superstition that produced fish. When it snagged in a tree, I wouldn't just yank hoping that it would come down. I would exit the river, reach high and try to pull down branches and, occasionally, trees to retrieve it.

And the fish it caught—I don't remember them all, but it caught palm-sized brookies, gnarled big browns and everything in between. First the tail fibers fell out. But somehow that was OK because the dubbing brushed back around the bend, making the body almost look like a comet. Then I bent the hook when I extracted it from a fish that sucked it down deep into its mouth. With my hemostats, I bent the hook back, but it was never the same. Nearly any fish that gave me a fight or that foul hooked would almost straighten the hook. Eventually, it couldn't stay dry even after a week off the water. The hackle fibers became brittle and looked like split ends on over-styled hair. Even though I stopped fishing with the fly, I kept it pinned to the top left corner of my fly box for months, like a rabbit's foot dangling from a teenager's rearview mirror.

The very first fly I tied was nearly two decades ago. Shane Heaps's dad had a cheap vise in his basement. Shane and I spent hours twirling sewing thread around a hook. We made a bee. It had exposed knots and uneven dubbing. We didn't leave room in the gap for the fish to find the hook. We didn't know any better so we took the bee up to Gordon's pond. Stock rainbows—small tasteless things that preferred corn and hamburger to native bugs—swam next to the water inlet. We dragged that bee behind a half-filled bubble until whole hunks of feather fell off in the water. The sky streaked, then darkened. Finally, a rainbow grabbed on—probably out of pity. We landed it, and in the process of pulling the bee out of the fish's mouth, the fly disintegrated back to just a hook. The finless fish had a worn down tail that looked like a paddle. We proudly ate him breaded and deep-fried.

I once hated the idea that flies, no matter how well constructed, aren't permanent, but now I like it. That unknown expiration date keeps a constant flow in and out of my fly box that ensures nothing grows stagnant. If I were Buddhist, I would say something about the importance of learning about impermanence. I would talk about the monks who construct elaborate sand mandalas only to destroy them (sometimes by dunking them in a river) when they finish. But I'm not a Buddhist; I'm barely an angler.

I packed the flies for the wedding in Ziploc bags and stifled the urge to leave the bags just a little open so they wouldn't suffocate. Pam thanked me with a hug, and I said it wasn't a big deal. I tried, but the truth is they weren't really for her or Nate. The flies I tie aren't even for the fish I catch. They're for me. They nurture whatever superstition I'm currently buying. I've lifted rocks and looked at what crawls out. They look a bit like my Pheasant Tails but nothing like my Purple Hazes.

The flies made the trip to the reception in Oregon, but I didn't. I imagine—I hope—the person who arranged the flies on the tables put them jutting out from flower arrangements, that they made it look like a confused mayfly attempted to pollinate roses or a black-and-gray sculpin was rushing around the rocks anchoring the flowers in the glass pitchers. More than that, I just hope they got out of their bags.

Rule 8

MAYBE YOUR STATURE AS A FLY FISHERMAN ISN'T DETERMINED BY HOW BIG A TROUT YOU CAN CATCH BUT BY HOW SMALL A TROUT YOU CAN CATCH WITHOUT BEING DISAPPOINTED (JOHN GIERACH)

How Small a Trout

Russ Beck

As we crossed into Montana, I saw two things: a school bus graveyard and lots of fishable water. Granted, I had traveled next to the Snake River in Idaho, but Montana's water seemed like my kind of water—bendy and shallow.

I was on my way to Missoula for an academic conference. My wife and our two-month-old daughter came along to visit my wife's sister. The conference center overlooked the Clark Fork River. As I sat listening to essays about authors I had never read, I thought about that water. And I took breaks, breaks much longer than I needed, by the river. I had been to Missoula before but had never fished there. In the car, buried beneath a stroller, Pack 'N Play and humidifier was my 4-weight, along with my vest filled with flies and my least-leaky waders.

I tried to resist, but in the weeks prior to the trip, I looked up Missoula fishing reports. These showed photographs of wiry men in baseball caps holding trout with two hands. Their faces smiled, but their teeth were gritted, making the trout look heavy.

I asked my brother-in-law to find me "a creek, preferably on private property, teeming with trout." What he gave me was the Bitterroot. There wasn't a good way to slip out on my own, so we all went—my wife, infant daughter, brother-in-law, sister-in-law and their two-year-old boy. We pulled

I tried to resist, but in the weeks prior to the trip, I looked up Missoula fishing reports. These showed photographs of wiry men in baseball caps holding trout with two hands. Their faces smiled, but their teeth were gritted, making the trout look heavy.

up to an underpass where columns supporting the highway wicked up the wide river. Leaning against the remnants of an old railroad bridge was a man in his mid-fifties with a potbelly and yellow sunglasses. He looked like what I imagine my dad would look like if he lived in Montana. I nodded a hello and kept walking.

"What are you going to use?" he asked.

"Hadn't decided yet."

"Well, come here then."

From the footings of the old bridge, we had a good view of the river. Two channels dug down with a sandbar in the middle.

"They're rising on both sides of the sandbar." He pointed with his whole hand. "And there seems to be a decent hatch happening."

"What's hatching?"

"Well, nothing has come up this high, but it looks like mostly caddis."

At the farmers' market that morning, I'd purchased a Goddard Caddis, tied with spun deer hair and two exaggerated antennae jutting out over the eye. I hoped that I would get to use it. I thanked the man for the advice, and he nodded.

As I walked away, he said, "Careful. This river will break your heart."

I helped my family get settled on camping chairs and asked again if it was OK that I was fishing. My wife whipped her wrist and told me, "Go, go." I walked into the water followed by my nephew, who wasn't wearing waders. I looked back to see my brother-in-law lift his son out of the river. The boy's shoes dripped cloudy water back into the river.

Fish rose everywhere, and in addition to the caddis hatch, a large rust-colored mayfly stumbled on the surface. Surprisingly, I could walk across the river without much trouble. I tried to anchor into the sandbar to fish both sides. Pods of what looked like eighteen-inchers gulped flies from the surface film. Their bodies seemed hefty as their dorsal fins broke the water's surface.

On the shore, my wife and her sister danced with their kids and took pictures while my brother-in-law tried to show his son how to skip rocks.

I started with the farmers' market caddis. I cast right to them. My flies almost snagged their backs. Nothing. I switched to an Adams. Nothing. I heard my leader snap as my casts became desperate and sloppy. Then I went subsurface. I saw one fish bend to let the current take him downstream, following my fly. He rose up. His pectoral fins pushed him closer. His nose nearly touched my fly. But nothing. I slapped my rod against the water and dug my heels into the sand. For a while I just watched the fish feed.

Eventually, I walked to the bank to get a soda and check in with my family. They didn't seem to notice I was there or that I had left. I watched my nephew throw rocks into the river to feel the water splash back on his face. My brother-in-law asked how it was going and I said, "Not good."

When I set the hook, the fish skipped across the surface of the water like a skipping stone. I netted the fish quickly, and my brother-in-law and nephew came to look at the haul.

"Well, there's been a guy jumping just over there for the last half hour—you should go get him."

I looked where he pointed and saw the erratic splashes of a small fish feeding just off the bank and upstream. I took off my vest and half-heartedly cast in. On my second cast, I connected with a trailing nymph. When I set the hook, the fish skipped across the surface of the water like a skipping stone. I netted the fish quickly, and my brother-in-law and nephew came to look at the haul.

"Fish?" my nephew asked.

"Well, technically," said my brother-in-law.

I chuckled and shrugged.

The rainbow lay in my hand. His tail tickled the tips of my fingers and his nose bumped my wrist. He had exaggerated fins and par marks that measured his length by quarter inches. This, clearly, was a fish that never fought for food in cement raceways.

"You can touch it," I said to the boy. He looked at me, his mouth forming a perfect O, but he didn't say anything. He reached out one finger and slid it across the slick body of the fish.

As the fish swam away, its small dorsal fin also broke the water's surface.

A Very Small Stream

Chadd VanZanten

When Mama Java sees me in my fishing get-up, she says, "Well. Look at you, fisherman."

I shrug. Mama sips her coffee.

"Did you sleep OK last night?" she asks.

"Yeah, it was great."

This is a lie.

"Oh, good," says Mama. "'Cuz those bunk beds can be iffy."

True.

"So," I say, "how do I get to this creek?"

"It's just down the hill," she says, pointing. "Go past the cabins and down the logging road until it ends. Then keep going."

"Any idea what the fishing's like?"

"Nah. It's pretty small. Very small, actually. But I know there's fish in it."

"Are they cutthroat? Do you know? Or brown trout?"

Mama frowns and shakes her head. "Oh, I don't know one fish from another."

We stand there for a moment, looking down the hill. Then I nod at Mama and start down the path. She goes inside.

Bleached-out slash and deadfall bar the way at the end of the logging road. I clamber over, gingerly, so I don't snag my waders. I come to a down-sloping meadow and then the going is easy. Gravity pulls me down the drainage until I find a trail. I follow my feet.

A hiker approaches but doesn't see me until I'm close enough to tap him with my rod. When he finally notices, he flinches and emits a squeak.

"God. Thought you were a bear or something."

I consider attacking him so he won't feel as embarrassed. He sidesteps me cautiously, as though maybe he's still unsure, and then he continues up the trail.

Soon I hear the water. It can't be that small. It's got some volume. I quicken my pace. My rod tip waggles like a divining rod.

Actually getting to the water is tougher. Undergrowth and fallen timber guard every bend. I collapse my rod and push through, ducking, turning sideways.

I back up, and when I push in again, there in the shade lies a sun-speckled riffle. Tall pines rise up on either side. I wade in. It's like stepping into a flooded cathedral. Birds are darting from branch to branch above me, contending, scolding. I walk upstream, not fishing yet. I see rise rings and an occasional splash.

They're brook trout.

Boulders and logs cradle the water, creating a chaotic staircase of quiet falls and stepped pools. There is little space for casting. I definitely didn't need the waders. I tie on a caddis pattern small enough for the brookies to eat but too big for them to miss. Those brookies—they always miss.

Just as Mama Java told me, it is a very small stream.

That the trout are also small is no surprise, then.

But they're there. They're practically everywhere. They're out in the open, midstream, so I float the fly right down the channel. Then I fish the edges and catch a few more. Then I fish the edges of the edges.

Not a single one is longer than the length of my hand, but these fish have me grinning and chuckling—the way they dart out from beneath the overhanging vegetation, how they rocket with blinding speed from my grasp as soon as they're unhooked.

I thought the caddisfly I tied on was small enough for these little brookies to get hold of—apparently not. They miss and miss. But no one can say they don't apply themselves. They gladly follow the fly down the drift to take two, three and sometimes four turns.

Not a single one is longer than the length of my hand, but these fish have me grinning and chuckling.

The end of the trip is a bend pool perhaps four feet deep with a sandy bottom. In it, a single brook trout is suspended just a few inches down, swimming stationary in the flow of the inlet and gulping forage from the surface every couple minutes.

It is oblivious, too, facing upstream without a care, with that big-eyed and lost expression that small fish seem to wear. I crouch in the shade a few yards downstream of the pool. The brookie doesn't seem to notice me.

"You haven't got a chance," I think.

But I don't cast to him, not just yet. Instead, I watch him for a minute or two, flashing in the sun. Then I sit down on the bank and try to work out how the tiny trout can hold his position so precisely with such economy of motion. It's mesmerizing.

The brook trout is there when I stand up to leave and still there when I clip my fly off the tippet and collapse my rod. Sometimes I can't tell one fish from another, either. I get out of the stream, take a few steps and then turn for one last look. The trout is still there, just a sleek figure silhouetted against the blond, sandy bottom of the pool.

ALWAYS TELL THE TRUTH SOMETIMES

ALWAYS TELL THE TRUTH SOMETIMES

Russ Beck

Here's a story that may or may not be true.

I went to a river up in Idaho that trickles nearly to a stop across a flat. Pools swirl around rocks. It's never deeper than a couple feet. Red willows hide the stream like a hedge maze. The main stem gets lost and breaks into smaller channels out of frustration. I tied on an elk-hair caddis, and on nearly every cast I caught a fish—little brookies that would dart out from under cut banks, rainbows that would snap at the fly when I pulled in line.

I would be lying if I said I never lied about fishing, but I know I'm in good company. When I tell people that I fish, they smile with just the corners of their mouths, lose eye contact with me and tell a story. Some of the stories are true. Everyone has a summer when they were a teenager that they spent near a lake/stream/river where they caught a record-breaking number of trout, glass-toothed muskies, enough bluegills to fill ten-gallon buckets and you-could-fit-your-fist-in-their-mouth bass. I smile and nod. I ask for specifics from those I don't believe. I'm not trying to trip them up or catch them in a lie. I just want to see how the story ends because I want to know how to end my lies, too.

Here's another story. It's probably not true.

Cream-colored mayflies about the size of nickels rose off the river in clouds.

We fished about a half mile down from the pump house on the Blacksmith Fork River. Even though there's a side channel that avoids the pump house, the fish still pile up in this section, making it often fished but still productive. The water is mostly riffles. The fish like to hug the banks, where the water's a little deeper, but when there's a hatch on, even a small one, the entire stretch boils.

That day, it boiled.

Cream-colored mayflies the size of nickels rose off the river in clouds. The three of us all tied on a different mayfly imitation and got nothing. We switched flies. Then we switched again. Brad stretched a seine over his landing net and found that, in addition to the mayflies, there was a small, black midge coming off. That must have been what they were feeding on.

We scoured our fly boxes for something small and black, but nothing really changed. Eventually, Brad broke away and fished the side channel. Chadd and I stayed on the main stem and hugged the banks to conceal our shadows. We cast to rising fish but had trouble connecting. I finally pulled in an eleven-inch brown on an all-black gnat, size-18. Chadd had a promising take that shook off. I pulled in another small fish and then lost my fly to a tree. We inched our way up to the pump house. Eroded yellow bricks patched with concrete attempt to contain the stream while water bubbles up from an unseen source against the house, making it look like an aerated aquarium. It's the last spot in the stretch that's convenient to fish. So, we tried, but we both felt defeated. I tried bow-and-arrow casts not out of necessity but out of boredom.

I think I may have been more surprised than the fish. Right up against the pump house a fish rose in the aerated water and smashed my Purple Haze. I set the hook. He broke my line instantly. I cursed my bad knots. Chadd climbed the bank and went to try somewhere else. Brad showed up while I tied on another fly. I flung it into the same mess, and again, a fish took the fly. My rod bent into a U, and Brad jumped down the bank to help me net the fish.

He wasn't the biggest fish but easily the biggest fish of the day. Plus, I was fishing using a tenkara rod, so his size felt exaggerated. He had a hump on his back just behind his head. I've been able to palm a basketball since I was twelve, but I couldn't fit my hand around him. I'm sure I would have lost him if Bradley hadn't been there with his net.

On the way back to the car, Brad said, "When you write about fishing, you should write about this, about today. Not catching anything where you should be catching—then pulling in that brown at the very end." I agreed it would make a good story.

But I'm not sure it would. It's too on the nose, too perfect. And if a *good* fishing story is defined by believability, nobody would believe that.

Here's another story, different day, different river, same disclaimer.

We edged up to the lip of the canyon and saw the tea-tinted water below. When we got out of the car, we were greeted by puffs of mayflies. Their question-mark bodies rose from the water and went off to wherever it is they go to harden up. The day was partly cloudy, which kept the temperature down. My hands shook with excitement as I tied on flies at the riverbank—everything seemed perfect.

But it wasn't.

I tried a combination of nymphs through great pockets but didn't even get a hit. I tried another combination and then another. I kept looking over

We edged up to the lip of the canyon and saw the tea-tinted water below.

my shoulder to see if my buddies were having any luck. Without warning, Brad caught a rainbow the size and shape of my forearm, a gorgeous fish that seemed to glow.

Eventually, Brad went down the canyon, and Chadd went up the canyon. I scrambled to higher ground and watched them both fish for a while. I used them like surveyors. I thought if I saw one pulling out fish, I'd go over by them. But neither did. So I lay in the sagebrush and tried to nap.

After a couple hours, we changed locations. We went to a place where we always have luck. It was better but not great. By the end of the day, I'd nearly made it to double digits, but I had expected more.

This story would be so much better if I moved the average fishing to the first of the story and ended with the crappy fishing only to have Brad catch that big old fish at the very end. It would give the average and poor fishing meaning—it was all in service of catching the rainbow. But that's not the way it happened because that's not the way it ever happens.

I teach writing at Utah State University in the offseason. I don't know how many times I've stood in front of my class drawing arcs on a whiteboard. I label the parts: "exposition," "rising action," "climax," "falling action." My pump house–trout story has all that. But it doesn't make a good fishing story. As demonstrated by Brad's rainbow story, fishing is actually all exposition and climax. Think about it: you fuel up the car, you drive to your location, you pull on your waders, you wade, you cast and you wade some more. YOU CATCH A FISH. You wade, and you wade some more.

When a fishing story follows the story arc too perfectly, something seems off. There's something not right about telling a true fishing story exactly as it happened. Maybe that's one reason we lie about fishing—because we need to make it less perfect. We need to give our stories a patina. Or we lie to keep up the romance. We hide how easy it is so more people won't do it and trudge through our fishing holes.

More than anything, we lie because we can't not lie. Even when I fish alone—when there's no one to lie to—I sometimes find myself fudging numbers in my head. Fishing necessitates lying because of what it is. Anglers have to imagine what happens under the water because of our terrestrial-only view. We patch over holes in our stories while they're happening. Anglers lie because even when they fish with other people, fishing is a solitary act.

The fly angler places the fly in the right current. He gets the perfect drift. He sees the fish turn and take.

And sometimes, it actually happens.

We've earned the stereotype of liars, but sometimes, I want people to believe me. And here's the catch—the more meticulous my notes of specific flies and catch totals, the less people believe me. When I lie, they think I'm lying. When I tell the truth, they know I'm lying. The most suspicious people are non-anglers or the occasional angler. I told a friend at work that I caught fifty fish (bluegills—they barely count) and saw her look at me sideways and giggle a little. I tried to explain that she could do it, too, that the bluegills were delirious and desperate, but she just walked away. As she did I said, "Maybe the number was closer to forty-five. I don't know." She didn't even turn around.

For this reason, I've pretty much stopped giving numbers when I talk about fishing trips. Instead, fish are measured in hand and arm lengths, catch totals are measured by meals and approximates ("less than fifteen, more than ten"). When I'm vague—even when I know the specific numbers and details—I feel more honest because so much of a fishing trip is guessed at anyway. Even though people don't believe me no matter what I do, I find I lie less the more I fish. My ability has nearly caught up to my lies. But occasionally, before I can catch myself, I let one of those fish in my head loose to swim around the ankles of my friends. But they're not big anymore. Well, not *that* big.

Here's the last one. It's all lies.

Again, I fished with Brad and Chadd on a small, technical stream on the tail end of the brown spawn. We took turns catching fish because there wasn't enough water for all three of us to fish at the same time. So, we watched and coached one another. I sat on a snowy bank and listened to Chadd whip roll casts into small currents. Brad stood at his left shoulder with a video camera. Chadd's indicator would bob and bounce down the river, sometimes impossibly slow. Then they went up and around a bend and left me alone. I looked for those perfect scars of clean gravel where the browns left their eggs and saw one under a pool my friend had underfished. I cast, and a brown lifted her head and took my egg pattern. I pulled her in silently, looked at her brilliant red spots and let her go before my friends noticed. When we walked back to the car, I didn't tell them about the fish I did or didn't catch.

Toward the Wilder Places

Chadd VanZanten

The chubby kid with the freckles isn't getting it. He hunches at his vise with his thread in the wrong hand, nose so close to the fly his eyes begin to cross. From where I'm standing, it looks like he's dropped all his feathers and is slowly lashing his own index finger to the shank of a fishhook.

"Jeremy," I say, "hold up. Jeremy, stop."

He can't hear me. I'm at front of the class, and around the table are five other junior fly tiers, each raising a racket such to wake Fredric Michael Halford himself from his very grave. We're tying the Wooly Bugger, so the tabletop lies beneath several inches of neon-colored marabou feathers. They're wispy and weightless, and they blow around in the commotion like debris in a typhoon. The flies are all dressed like tiny drag queens. This one's got a misshapen body of hot pink with orange tail. That one has black chenille with sky-blue hackle.

Jeremy leans closer to the vise and his eyes cross alarmingly.

"Jeremy," I holler. Then I think maybe his name isn't Jeremy.

"Jacob."

No response. All I know for sure is that it's a J name.

"Jason. Jared. Jeff." He keeps winding.

I can't just shout, "Hey, fat kid in the blue shirt," so I walk over to his tying station and take the bobbin from him as gently as I can.

"Tell me your name again. Jason? James?"

"Skylar," he says.

"Seriously."

Skylar raises his eyebrows and nods, as if it's something of a surprise to him, too.

I hand the bobbin back to him and say, "Skylar, this goes in your other hand." He forms an O with his mouth.

It's a three-day fly-fishing camp for twelve-year-olds sponsored by my chapter of Trout Unlimited. We teach them how to tie, how to cast, how to fish. A few of them know a little about fly-fishing. Most know nothing about everything. They move from class to class like a small and barely contained circus, becoming only a little quieter when the instruction begins.

Skylar unravels his botched fly and starts over, but all the feathers fall off again. He looks at me.

"You gotta keep it tight," I say. "That's what I've been trying to tell you."

He leans forward. His eyes cross again, and his tongue slides out of the corner of his mouth as he winds the thread, tighter this time. The feathers stay on.

When we finish up, there's marabou all over everything and everybody. The kids clean up, kind of, and I shoo them on to the next class. Everywhere they go, we tell them to keep things tight—tight thread, tight loops, tight lines.

That's because at the center of fly-fishing, you will find only tension—harnessed and modulated, then applied. A fly is little more than a moment of time wrapped into a tight and complicated knot. The cast is a nylon line drawn taut by energy stored for a split second in a fly rod. Tension between molecules bears the fly up on the surface of the water and carries it downstream to the trout. And the angler who does not understand the importance of maintaining tension on the line after a trout takes the fly is not yet an angler.

My neighbor Rick once asked me, "So, you're into fly-fishing?"

I shrug. "That's certainly one way of putting it."

"I've always wanted to try it. Is it relaxing? It looks relaxing."

"No," I answer, "not really."

"Oh," he says. Then he looks at the ground.

It's true. Fly-fishing is about tension, not slack. On the big tail waters—the Missouri, the Green—fly-fishing is seldom serene. In the wide-open and indifferent water, there are beefy, torpedo-like trout whose sole purpose seems to lie in making grown men feel inadequate, irrelevant. These are not places for relaxation. The smaller streams are but a little more accommodating, with their brushy, technical lanes and ever-changing moods.

When you fly fish, you fly fish. That's all. If you wish to relax, drink beer, nap or consider your place in the cosmos, you must stop casting. And when you begin to cast again, you have to come to attention, clear your mind. Fly-fishing may hold some association with relaxation and thought experiments on the meaning of existence but only because these pursuits become easier once the trip is over.

I didn't explain any of this to Rick that day, didn't even try, because there is also tension between the angler and those around him. When the angler tries to tell his family or neighbors about the last fish he caught, they nod absently or change the subject. They do not understand. Many anglers can scarcely abide the company of other anglers. For Sartre, hell is other people; for fly anglers, hell is other fly anglers. Certainly, they can't be made responsible for enlightening the unwashed, too.

Then there are the wives, the girlfriends, those ladies who wait for their angler-men. The man who fishes and claims things are never tense between himself and the woman in his life is either a liar or a bastard. From her perspective, the matter is very simple: "If he spends more time fishing than he spends with me, then fishing is more important to him than I am."

No angler has ever managed to disprove this equation.

Saturday morning arrives. I throw my rod and waders in the truck. My wife appears on the back steps and asks, "When will I see you?"

"Oh, I dunno," I say, acting as if I hadn't thought about it until just then. "Three thirty. Maybe four."

"Which means five or five thirty."

Actually, I'm thinking seven or eight, but I don't tell her that. Instead, I pause by the truck and say, "Well, when do you want me home?"

"I don't want you home at any certain time. I'm asking. When will I see you?"

We watch each other for a few seconds across the driveway, her with arms folded, me grasping the door handle of the truck.

"It depends," I answer. "I'm thinking no later than five thirty, six."

"See you at seven." She goes inside.

Eight it is.

I pull away from the house and try not to drive too fast. The responsibilities of home and office protest. Every stoplight takes so long I convince myself that the town's entire traffic-control system is malfunctioning.

Then I reach the canyon and begin to climb. At certain bends in the highway, I steal glances at the water. There is nothing I can learn from a half-second glimpse at a river fifty yards down a ravine, except maybe that it is still where I left it, but I keep looking anyway.

Depending on the timing of the trip and what there is for me to do at home, there may be a twinge of guilt as I leave town, but it's soon squelched. There is in every canyon a demarcation beyond which the everyday world no longer has any influence over me. After that, I feel only the constant gravity that pulls us all toward the wilder places.

And so at last, there is tension between the angler and the stream. It's a little like the electricity between two rivals. The stream necessarily stands as a challenge to the angler, who has come to unlock her secrets—streams do not give those up easily. To step into the water is to accept the challenge. But it is also like the tension between lovers. Waiting to enter the stream is like waiting for the touch of a lover's hand.

I park, pull on my waders and hike down a trail to the bank. Swallows dive and swoop over the stream, picking off insects as they drift up and into the sunlight. I step into the stream. I accept her challenge, feel her touch.

The tension increases, pulling in all directions at once. The current, temperature, time of day—everything's good. There will be fish today, a lot of them. I situate myself among the rocks and cast to a slender ribbon of smooth water, the seam between fast and slow currents.

I feel only the constant gravity that pulls us all toward the wilder places.

A trout gulps the fly. The tension does not dissipate, but it shifts. It equalizes. I lift my rod tip, and the line comes tight to the trout. I feel his soft weight on the line.

Appendix A

ON VARIOUS CATCH TOTALS AND THEIR SIGNIFICANCE, BY CHADD VANZANTEN

I

The first fish answers "no" to the question of whether you will be skunked today and, therefore, is always welcome. The number-one fish takes you over a divide of sorts. You have readied yourself for fishing, and you begin to cast.

The first fish answers "No" to the question of whether you will be skunked today and, therefore, is always welcome.

But without at least one fish, all you really have to do is stop casting for a moment, and you're back at the first step again. You might as well be in your driveway, still trying to find a good song to start the drive. After the first fish is in your net, you are on to a third step, one that validates your preparation and driving tune selection.

If you're in a place where fish are hard to come by, your first catch will represent a gulf between those who caught that day and those who did not. And when fishing in a group, of course, it's hard to overstate the satisfaction that comes when *your* first fish is *the* first fish.

For me, the first fish often makes its appearance right away, on an early cast, maybe because my focus is so thorough but more probably because I haven't had time to spoil the entire stream yet.

II

The second fish confirms what you're always hoping: that the first one wasn't a fluke. You have at least managed to get it right twice, meaning there's a fair chance that you could do it a third time.

When fishing in very productive waters, you might blow past that second fish without pausing. I advise against this. Take note of the number-two fish and salute him, lest he be lost among the other fish you catch that day.

III

Fish number three lends a certain Izaak Walton completeness to your catch, especially if you are fishing for supper. Three good fish, lying picturesquely on a bed of grass in a wicker creel, are enough to feed yourself and your protégé, with something left over for the milkmaid.

IV

No one considers the fourth fish significant. Some fish will simply escape notice. The sixth, for example. Fish number seven, along with thirteen, may be interesting if you're superstitious. But no one pays attention to, say, the eleventh or twenty-third fish.

There is something great about counting up fish by fives, even the ones you haven't caught yet.

V

The number-five fish is looked for because with it, you can report your catch by holding up all the fingers on one hand while maintaining a cool, trout-stalking reticence. The fifth fish also allows extrapolation. "It's 2:15, and I have five fish. If this keeps up, I could wind up with fifty by 8:30." There is something great about counting up fish by fives, even the ones you haven't caught yet.

VI

The tenth fish is a benchmark for obvious reasons. You can just grunt, "Got ten" at your buddy. That's got a nice ring, especially if the trip was somewhat short or the fish somewhat long. You're now also into double digits, which gives you an option of describing the day in those terms. For example, if your buddy says, "Thirty-five; how'd you do?" you may now answer, "I got into double digits, too."

VII

Fish number twelve allows you to use the word "dozen."

VIII

Hello, twenty, thirty and forty. There are fewer and fewer places in the world where ordinary anglers can catch twenty fish and not consider that a good trip. Twenty fish make a day memorable even if your buddy catches forty. I often make twenty my goal, though on an "ordinary" day, several factors have to fall into place to reach that number, and going beyond it strikes me as relentless. The number-twenty fish seems to ask me, "Don't you have anything better to do with your time?" to which I answer, "No, not really."

Some calibration may be in order here. If your home water is a bluegill pond, twenty fish is the opening act. If you fish steelhead, thirty fish may be a month's work.

A few years ago I got a fish counter in the shape of a little rainbow trout with a dial and a tiny window that reads from "01" to "00." I thought it would be fun for the few places where I'm in danger of catching more fish than I can count in my head, but whenever I used it, my catch totals seemed depressed. I once brought it to Montana to fish on what was supposed to be a dynamite trout stream. At the end of the day, the counter read "09." The next day, I left it in the tent and caught twenty-seven. I've never fished with it again. When it comes to fishing and jinxes, that's as close to hard science as a fly angler needs.

IX

What can be said about the fiftieth fish? If you're holding the number-fifty fish, either the fish are just a bunch of butt-kissers or you have moved into a hazy, euphoric state of mind we sometimes refer to as "the zone," where practice and experience dim the clamor of the conscience mind and tap into some primitive place in the brainstem where nothing exists but your efforts and their object.

My first memory of the zone is playing Galaga at an arcade decades ago. Fishing and Galaga actually have a lot in common. Both typically involve considerable profanity, for instance. Both involve complex sequences of motions repeated mechanically, interspersed with furious improvisation. And both will take you into the zone. I had blasted my way through the high score on the machine and racked up four or five extra lives when I noticed how relaxed my movements were and the way I anticipated my enemy's attacks three and four steps in advance. As I breezed through a Challenge Stage in the high twenties, I understood only that something up in my brain was different, sharper, better. Unfortunately, as soon as I became consciously aware of it, everything downshifted, the sharpness faded and my starfighter disintegrated in a cloud of eight-bit graphics and sound.

In his excellent resource *Zen in the Art of Archery*, the philosopher mystic Eugene Herrigel explains the zone this way: "This state of unconscious is realized only when, completely empty and rid of the self, he becomes one with the perfecting of his technical skill, though there is in it something of a

The number-one-hundred fish will shine and shimmer the same way the first one did. It will feel vibrant in your hand.

quite different order which cannot be attained by any progressive study of the art." When it comes to fishing small streams in Idaho, I have become convinced that the "something of a quite different order" Herrigel mentions is in fact twenty-two ounces of Dr. Pepper and a package of those little chocolate-covered donuts they always sell at gas stations.

X

Fish number one hundred. I was speaking in partly hypothetical terms about catching fifty fish at a single go—I visit that neighborhood periodically but can't afford to live there. Anything I say about catching one hundred fish is pure speculation. Let's say I've gotten a look at the neighborhood, but just from the highway.

Hypothetically, one hundred fish would be a lot of fun, but I doubt I'd have the expertise or discipline to keep fishing long enough to find out. Assuming I found a stream with such abundance, and further assuming I caught a fish every five minutes or so, I'd need to fish for more than eight hours to arrive at one hundred.

Even though such waters are uncharted for me, I suppose I can say one thing with certainty: the number-one-hundred fish won't be that different from the first, second or tenth. The number-one-hundred fish will shine and shimmer the same way the first one did. It will feel vibrant in your hand.

THE ESSAY IN WHICH THE AUTHOR COMPARES PEOPLE TO TROUT, BY RUSS BECK

I nearly turned back when I realized I forgot my sunglasses. Then I saw I was low on gas. Then I saw the river was packed with anglers. But I kept driving because I had to fish. I drove until I saw no one; then I drove another mile.

I had to fish because it was my favorite season, and it doesn't last long: late summer, early fall; after Labor Day, before Halloween; just when it's getting cooler but far from cold. I put in downstream from a beaver pond that didn't exist a month earlier. The cows had done their best to rid the hills of vegetation, but the remaining grass appeared golden. Willows and scrub oaks guarded the river on both sides. Everything smelled dusty and brittle. There wasn't a visible hatch, but the water rippled with takes.

Around this time, it seems that fish feel some desperation. They sense the cold coming and the winter that won't yield too many bugs to the surface, and they know that they'll have to take things they wouldn't have weeks before.

Within a few casts, I had my first fish. A small cutthroat whose slits under his chin glowed hunter orange. The cutties seemed to have brightened up like the scrub oak that lines the river. They all seemed shiftless like me—especially the young ones. They darted from hole to hole and used much more energy than needed to take bugs off the surface. My next fish came out of the water for my Adams. His mouth anchored to the fly, and his tail wheeled around like the hands of a clock and splashed into the still water

I've had days when I couldn't keep little brookies off the hook and, once, a day when I couldn't keep off little browns. This was the first time that I couldn't keep off cutts. They competed for nearly every fly cast. Most were small, but some were respectable. The other days didn't feel that satisfying. I

Rainbow trout remind me of the rich lawyers and doctors who retired in my little hometown and bought up land where I once moved irrigation pipes in alfalfa fields.

became complacent about catching fish—I began to expect the fish instead of hoping for them, which ruins the whole ethos of fishing.

But not on the cutthroat day—it was the best fishing I had that year.

It's because I like cutthroats the best, partly because they're native. The ancestors of the fish I caught were here long before my ancestors, and I don't mean my great-great-grandpa or even white guys. I mean humans.

But more than that, they're just my favorite.

Rainbow trout remind me of the rich lawyers and doctors who retired in my little hometown and bought up land where I once moved irrigation pipes in alfalfa fields. They build garish mansions decorated with stuff from Pottery Barn. They run for local office, get seats on the boards and change zoning laws. They own successful businesses—for fun. They're charming and nice. If I still lived there, I think I'd try to organize a poker night with a handful of them. You almost believe they've always been there and that they belong.

Brookies always show up late. You can trace your finger across maps on their backs, and they somehow lead you east. I imagine even their kids talk with Boston accents, even though they've been living in the West for generations. On a Sunday, they're as comfortable reading Whitman as they

You can trace your finger across maps on their backs, and they somehow lead you east. I imagine even their kids talk with Boston accents even though they've been living in the West for generations.

are cheering for the Pats. At parties, people eventually form circles around them. They tell stories about their uncle who, because he didn't have a better idea, threw all his loose change up into his attic. After forty years, the ceiling beams sagged and creaked. The cache became an accidental retirement fund. When the story ends, the brook trout will quiet down and wait. He'll wait because he's polite and he wants to hear a story, but when no one starts in, he'll tell you another. He fidgets and talks too much with his hands. He says that when he was a teenager he drank a bottle of off-brand coffee liquor and met a famous rock star in an elevator.

The trout was, of course, famously drunk and recognized the rock star but could only shout at him in the small confines of an elevator, "Jesus, you're short. Like really short!" You want to buy the storyteller—and the uncle and maybe even the rock star—a beer. But when you offer, brookies just smile and say no, they've got some place to be.

Brown trout somehow know everyone in town. They're either related to them or went to elementary school together or something. And these tendrils of relation are usually an embarrassment to either the trout or the person they know. They clog the once-quiet trails with their ATVs. They fly by in a cloud of dust, Mountain Dew cans and cigarette boxes. The girls are waitresses at diners, where they wear too much eye makeup, and the boys

They're just good folk with clean, calloused hands. If you need some woodwork done in your house, you'd call one of them. You'd let them date your daughter. He'll call you "Sir" or "Ma'am" and have her home ten minutes before curfew.

I wanted to know which fish they'd catch.

do whatever they can to pay down the debt they can't dodge. They're not pariahs, but they're approaching that. They're folk you'd tell your nephew to avoid, and you'd never buy one of their used cars.

You wouldn't buy a used car from a cutthroat either, but that's because he would run it into the ground and not sell it. Instead, he'd retire it to a field on a farm, promising to come back for it someday when he had more cash to restore it. And although he meant it, the car will sit in the field for years—up on blocks and clean. They're a handsome fish, with their almost-bronze coloring and muddy splotches. They're just good folk with clean, calloused hands. If you need some woodwork done in your house, you'd call one of them. You'd let them date your daughter. He'll call you "Sir" or "Ma'am" and have her home ten minutes before curfew.

On the way home from the cutthroat day, I pulled over and watched three older anglers wet wade. This late in the season, the water is shallow and gentle, but they still held onto one another's shoulders for stability. Although their rods moved back and forth slowly, the line listened and their loops unfolded like quilts being shaken out for summer storage. I sat and watched for longer than I should have.

I waited for one of them to catch a fish because I wanted to know which fish they'd catch.

A PARTIAL CHECKLIST FOR FISHING ALONE, BY CHADD VANZANTEN AND RUSS BECK

Cameras: It seems since we no longer keep fish, we need photographs of fish—as proof, maybe. We hold the fish out to make them appear larger. We pucker up and slap a kiss on the snout of a trout. But that's not what the camera is really for. Because if you need to prove that you caught fish when you fish alone, then you need to rethink, well, everything. The camera, the phone—whatever—is there to pollute your quotidian data with rivers, mountains and fish so that when you're working on whatever it is you work on, you'll stumble across that photograph of the scrub oak in full fall orange or the one of that fish wiggling out of your fishing buddy's hands. It works as a tether, connecting you back to the river. It's also there when you're on the river and need a reminder of what's at home waiting for you. Otherwise, some days, you might not come home.

A hat: So that you can take it off and rub your forehead when it's all just too goddamned pretty.

Something new: If you're not experimenting while you fish alone, you're not doing it right. Try that putty stuff as a strike indicator.

Yarn strike indicator: That putty stuff really doesn't work.

Strike indicators: The kind you used before. If it's not broke, don't fix it.

Whiskey: Not entirely necessary, until it is.

A book: Put it in your pack. You'll read it exactly twice during the summer while fishing. It's not for reading. It will double as a pillow when you take a nap in the river. (The preposition "in" is not an error. It's essential that you lie with your torso on the bank and your legs in the water. This will ensure the best nap of the summer.)

An arsenal of old junk: Rusty flies, brittle leaders, dry-rotted boot-foot neoprene waders and everything else you don't use anymore. Your outdated gear is a trophy room. It's where you came from, what worked and what didn't and what needs to be tried again. You also need loaner gear for that guy at work who insists that he wants to fish—reach into that stockpile, grab an armful and pile it on him. Remember, someone did that for you. Plus, if you're lucky, the guy from work won't make you go with him.

Audio distraction: A book on tape, music or something. This, perhaps more than any other item on this list, will be disputed. The argument is that in order to commune with Mother Nature, one must be unencumbered by the distractions of civilization. One must hear the bright gurgle of the stream, feel the downstream breeze, catch the delicate bouquet of pond scum. I argue that you have plenty of time and ways to connect with nature. She's a pushy broad. My favorite audiobook on baking includes a section in which the author explains that when she first started baking, she avoided using electric mixers. She states that she wanted to be one with the kneading process, but she later admits that she found plenty of opportunities to communicate with the yeast without always having her fingers in the dough. I suggest that listening to something while fishing will actually enhance your perception of the river. It's like an artist learning to paint by forcing herself to turn the photograph upside-down and concentrating on shapes rather than complete images. I want to keep going with this argument, but I think I'm losing.

A bad attitude: Allow fishing to be transformative. My favorite thing to do is go fishing when I'm in a bad place and to fish until I'm not in a bad place. Get pissed that you don't catch fish—you'll eventually catch a fish and feel all that weird anger sink through your feet and pollute the river.

Stuff for safety: Headlamp. When you're alone, the sun will abandon you, you will be three miles from the truck and it will be utterly dark. It's also useful for finding a fly box or hemostats dropped in the dusk. Also, extra food, in case you get stranded. Water. Put your cellphone in a waterproof bag and keep it with you. Important note—make sure you forget all of these.

An excuse: Either to get off the river if you're not feeling it or to keep you there longer if you are feeling it in excess. Last summer, one of my favorite places to fish was pocked with road construction. They were burying electrical lines or water or something. This worked for both excuses.

Bass gear: None of your buddies will bass fish with you anymore because they have something against "stagnant, stinky pond water." So it will become something you do secretly. Break out a float tube and fish in the glass-still pond. After catching fifty bluegills, your palm will sting with the punctures that accompany handling the fish from the Centrarchidae family. Once in the pond, you'll wonder why you don't do this more often. You'll think of the tales you'll tell your friends. You'll think, "The pond smell isn't that bad." You'll say, "Those campers with their four-wheelers and country music are almost endearing." "And the old ladies?" you'll conclude, "the ones in the lawn chairs chewing tobacco, watching you strip off your waders only to be disappointed when there are more pants under the water pants? They are, at worst, harmless." Then, when you go back to the streams and feel the smooth body of that first cutthroat, you'll ask, "What was I doing fishing in that pond?" Remember to put the cutthroat back in the stream.

The back seat of your car or the bed of your truck: Someplace you can dump your muddy, wet waders and boots. It's essential to cultivate the sweet, pungent smell of mildew.

Someone to fish with: Learning to fish alone requires someone else. Sit back and watch your buddy cast perfectly into exactly the right drift. Watch the netting of a trout by someone who is not you. And when that trout is large and heavy, you will need to net it for him. Do not be jealous. There are trout enough for all. But he sort of lucked into those last few, didn't he? It's OK to be a little annoyed. Wait, he knows about that spot behind the log that you never fish when he comes along? Yep. Caught another one there. You know, he can be such a prick sometimes. Look at him. Caught a sixteen-incher. Oh my hell. Another one? This is the whole entire goddamn reason you fish alone—and the unsolicited kibbutzing, the derailments of your trains of thought. You're the one who showed him this stretch. He practically stepped on the brown you would have obviously cast to. But he needs it more today.

He mentioned something about work sucking him dry and yadda yadda. Did he? Did he just pull that one out from under that bank? That cast was perfect. He hit in the only place that would connect. You want to still be mad, but, well, you can't. You didn't fish as much as you would have without him, but your arm is still sore. You'll buy at the taco truck tonight. It's important to have someone to talk to on the way back to town so that you're not always so goddamn alone.

ABOUT THE AUTHORS

Russ Beck received the Frederick Mannford Award for creative writing from the Western Literature Association. He edits and contributes to both howsmallatrout.wordpress.com and braidedbrook.com. He teaches writing at Utah State University. This is his first book.

Chadd VanZanten's essays on fly-fishing appear in the online fly-fishing journal *Eat Sleep Fish* and in The History Press anthology *Utah Reflections*. His short fiction can be found in *Between Places*, an anthology of poetry and prose by LUW Press. Chadd lives in Logan, where he works as a professional editor. When he is not writing, he is fishing. The opposite is also true.

Visit us at
www.historypress.net
....
This title is also available as an e-book